The Relationship Principles of Jesus g------ ------ practical tools to transform our relationships into all that God desires them to be. By pointing us to Jesus, Tom Holladay teaches us how to live the Christian life as it was really intended. Every follower of Jesus should take this forty-day journey, savoring each insight and applying it to every relationship they have.

DR. KEVIN LEMAN, author of *Have a New Kid by Friday*

I have had the honor of serving with Tom Holladay on the pastoral staff at Saddleback Church for the last sixteen years. He is a friend and accountability partner. Tom is a true example of how to live the relationship principles of Jesus.

JOHN BAKER, pastor and founder of Celebrate Recovery

Life's greatest joys and life's greatest pains are experienced in relationships. This book can help mitigate the pain and enhance the joy.

GARY D. CHAPMAN, PhD, author of *The Five Love Languages*

Our generation craves close, intimate relationships, but we're imperfect people who can't seem to get what we want most. *The Relationship Principles of Jesus* centers us on what matters most, giving practical wisdom and daily doses of encouragement we all need to better love those around us.

JOHN BURKE, author of *No Perfect People Allowed*

No one communicates better on this topic of Christlike relationships than Tom Holladay, who walks the talk. A must-read for anyone who is passionate about becoming more like Jesus — today.

KATIE BRAZELTON, PhD, MDiv, author of *Pathway to Purpose for Women*

The Relationship Principles of Jesus could revolutionize your relationships with God and with others. This book provides the essential ingredients to deepen and strengthen every relationship in your life.

DR. GARY SMALLEY, author of *Change Your Heart, Change Your Life*

Also by Tom Holladay

Foundations (coauthored with Kay Warren)

Love-Powered Parenting (coauthor with Chaundel Holladay)

Putting it Together Again When It's All Fallen Apart

THE
RELATIONSHIP
PRINCIPLES
OF
JESUS

TOM HOLLADAY

Teaching Pastor, Saddleback Church

ZONDERVAN

The Relationship Principles of Jesus
Copyright © 2008 by Tom Holladay

Requests for information should be addressed to:

Zondervan, 3900 Sparks Dr. SE, Grand Rapids, Michigan 49546

ISBN 978-0-310-35177-1 (softcover)

ISBN 978-0-310-30934-5 (audio)

ISBN 978-0-310-32056-2 (ebook)

Library of Congress Cataloging-in-Publication Data

Holladay, Tom, 1956-
    The relationship principles of Jesus / Tom Holladay.
      p. cm.
    ISBN 978-0-310-28367-6 (hardcover, jacketed)
    1. Interpersonal relations—Religious aspects—Christianity. I. Title.
  BV4597.52.H65   2008
  232.9'03—dc22   2008026328

Published in association with Rosenbaum & Associates Literary Agency, Brentwood, Tennessee.

Interior design by Beth Shagene

First printing June 2018 / Printed in the United States of America

The list of those who have formed, fashioned, and flavored
what is written in this book
would quickly grow to pages.
Relationships with family, coworkers, small group members,
children, and church family
have all played a part.

Amidst all of those human relationships,
there is far and away one person
from whom I've learned more about relationships than any other.
This book is dedicated with grateful joy to my wife, Chaundel.

Contents

RELATIONSHIP PRINCIPLE #1

Place the Highest Value on Relationships

> Jesus answered [the teacher of the law], "The most important command is this: 'Listen, people of Israel! The Lord our God is the only Lord. Love the Lord your God with all your heart, all your soul, all your mind, and all your strength.' The second command is this: 'Love your neighbor as you love yourself.' There are no commands more important than these."
>
> **Mark 12:29–31 NCV**

As You Judge, You Will Be Judged

> Do not judge, or you too will be judged. For in the same way you judge others, you will be judged, and with the measure you use, it will be measured to you.
>
> **Matthew 7:1-2**

The Greatest Are the Servants

> The greatest among you will be your servant. For whoever exalts himself will be humbled, and whoever humbles himself will be exalted.
>
> **Matthew 23:11-12**

RELATIONSHIP PRINCIPLE #6

Treat Others as You Want Them
to Treat You

Do to others as you would have them do to you.

Luke 6:31

Foreword

If I asked you what your #1 goal in life is, what would be your answer? Happiness? Success? Wealth? Comfort? Fame? To have fun? To be respected? Your answer would reveal your *dominant life value*. Everyone has a dominant life value, whether they realize it or not. You have one. It's what you unconsciously base your decisions on.

If your dominant life value is having fun, when choosing between two events, you'll naturally choose the one that's more fun. If your dominant life value is comfort, you'll tend to choose what's most comfortable for you. If it's safety, you'll choose the least risky alternative. If it's being appreciated, you'll do what gets you the most recognition.

God tells us that our dominant life value is *love*. Because God is love, and because he created you to love you, he wants you to learn to love too. Learning to love is the #1 lesson God intends for you to learn here on earth. Life is the school of love. Jesus once said that the entire Bible can be summed up in two commands: Love God with all your heart and love your neighbor as yourself (Matthew 22:37–39).

In fact, every one of the New Testament writers taught that learning to love God and each other is the most important lesson God expects us to learn. Paul wrote, *"Let love be your highest goal"* (1 Corinthians 14:1 NLT). John wrote, *"We know that we have passed from death to life, because we love our brothers. Anyone who does not love remains in death"* (1 John 3:14). James wrote, *"If you really keep the royal law found in Scripture, 'Love your neighbor as yourself,' you are doing right"* (James 2:8). Peter wrote, *"Most important of all, continue to show deep love for each other, for love covers a multitude of sins"* (1 Peter 4:8 NLT).

Learning to love God and others is to be our highest goal, our greatest aim, our first priority, our deepest aspiration, our strongest ambition, our constant focus, our passionate intention, and the dominant life value of our lives. The more we learn to how to *love authentically*, the more like Jesus we become.

This book is written by someone who has modeled genuine love to others for his entire adult life. For over thirty-five years, I've closely watched how Tom Holladay lives and leads by showing Christlike love to everyone, so I felt very fortunate when he married my sister. With his incredible grasp of both the Scriptures and human nature, Tom is eminently qualified to teach and write on this profound theme. For the nearly twenty years Tom has been a teaching pastor at Saddleback Church, tens of thousands of Saddleback members have been blessed by his insights into relationships. And hundreds of thousands of pastors have been trained by Tom as he and I have traveled the world together. This man has much to say, and you'll be blessed if you listen to him!

The opening sentence of *The Purpose Driven Life* is *"It's not about you."* This book, *The Relationship Principles of Jesus*, is a natural extension of that concept. Selfishness must be replaced by unselfishness. Conceit must be replaced by compassion. Ego must be replaced by altruism. The focus on "me" must give way to "we." It's all about loving God and others.

But how? In our fallen world where every heart and relationship is marred, broken, and damaged by sin, how can we apply the healing power of authentic love? This book points the way. Learning to love unselfishly is not an easy task. It runs counter to our self-centered nature. Only Jesus can teach us the kind of love that heals, restores, and deepens relationships. And only Jesus can give us the power to love that way.

The Relationship Principles of Jesus deals with the second of *Five Renewals* I deeply believe are needed in our culture and world. The first book, *The Purpose Driven Life*, focused on **personal renewal**. This is the starting point. Everything starts in the heart. Only changed people can change the world. The foundation for everything is getting to know and love God and serving his five purposes for your life.

But you were never meant to live your life in a vacuum. In fact, you cannot fulfill your life's purposes by yourself. You need other people's help, and they need yours. We're better together. This second kind of renewal, **relational renewal**, is what this book is all about. You must not only learn to love God with all your heart (personal renewal); you must learn to love your neighbor as yourself (relational renewal.)

With conflict, divorce, violence, prejudice, abuse, division, and polarization around us daily, it's obvious we all need some lessons in building healthy relationships. This is my dream: If every group and church that participated in the 40 Days of Purpose campaign worldwide would also study this book as a part of the 40 Days of Love campaign, it could bring about a revival of love that would change the cultural climate of our world. It can start with you.

Please write us at Love@purposedriven.com and tell us your story!

RICK WARREN
The Purpose Driven Life

Introduction

How do we bridge the relationship gap—the gap between
what we hope for and desire and what we actually experience?

On one side of the gap is the reality of failed marriages,
absent parents, rebellious children, disloyal friends, and
gossiping churches. On the other side of this gap place
the words of Jesus: "A new command I give you: Love one
another. As I have loved you, so you must love one another"
(John 13:34). When I look at how big this gap really is, I can
easily work myself into a Grand Canyon-sized depression.
How is it possible to ever bridge such a distance?

When you're in trouble, you need an expert. If you're
having problems with your kitchen sink, call a plumber; if
your car's transmission is going out, go see a mechanic. What
about relationships? Who is the expert? The world's foremost
expert on relationships is Jesus Christ. Just look at the way he
related to people. Jesus was *great* at relationships. The crowds
flocked to him, his followers loved to be around him, and even
his enemies paid him an unintended compliment when they
called him a "friend of ... 'sinners'" (Matthew 11:19).

A few years ago I sat down to read through the Gospels with an eye on relationships. I was looking for the answer to a simple question: How did Jesus relate to the thousands of people he came into contact with during his public ministry? I must honestly say I was quite surprised. The relationship expert did not always relate to others as I would have expected him to. Where I might have rebuked, he offered forgiveness (for example, Luke 7:36–50). Where I might have encouraged, he served up a scathing indictment (for example, Matthew 8:23–27). As I looked to learn about relationships from the example of Jesus, I felt a little like a middle school algebra student thrown into a university trigonometry class. I was in over my head. Sometimes I had to admit I didn't even understand the questions, let alone the answers. As one who had pastored and counseled people for many years, this came as a humbling experience. It wasn't that I was naive to the point of thinking I always did the right thing in relationships. But I thought I at least *knew* the right thing to do. I found that rather than just reinforcing our way of doing relationships, Jesus charts out an entirely new way of relating to people.

When Jesus says, "Turn the other cheek" (see Matthew 5:39), he points to a new way of relating to people. His stern challenges to Peter plot a new course in relationship skills. Would you or I chastise someone who had just walked on water for his lack of faith (see Matthew 14:31)? His sharp-tongued indictment of the Pharisees takes our old maps off the table. Most of us would consider it definitely unchristian to call others snakes (Matthew 23:33)! Jesus had a different way of relating to people, and we obviously have much to learn.

As I took the journey of reading through the Gospels, gradually and steadily six relationship principles emerged. These are the principles we'll focus on for the next forty days. I don't claim or intend this to be an exhaustive list, yet these six all-encompassing truths are seen again and again in Jesus' life and teaching.

Let's get a few things on the table from the start. First, these are clearly not the only principles Jesus gave us with regard to relationships. We could easily come up with a list of twenty or thirty relationship principles taught by Jesus. Yet these six are at the core of his teaching and his example.

Second, Jesus is the expert here — not any one of us, and that certainly includes me! We are fellow learners who look together at the expert — at Jesus — so we can learn from him.

The world's foremost expert on relationships is Jesus Christ.

As you open this book, you'll see forty chapters to be read over forty days. I strongly encourage you to read this book as it is laid out. The book is shaped this way because we tend to learn best over time and through repetition and reminders. You could choose to speed through this book in a few days, but it will not have nearly the impact on your relationships as will result over the course of forty days.

At the end of each day's reading, you'll find three features to help you in this journey. First, a Point to Ponder, which sums up the chapter's main message in a sentence. Second, a Verse to Remember, which gives a verse from the Bible that you can put to memory. Not many of us will be able to memorize a verse for each day, yet if you could choose just one of the verses from each week and memorize it, you'll be spiritually refreshed and strengthened in surprising ways. At the end of each chapter is also a Question to Consider — a personal thought question to focus your thinking toward action and change. At the end of the book, there is a list of additional Questions for Friends, Couples, and Small Groups. You'll learn more if you read this book at the same time as someone else, and then get together to share what you've both learned. These questions are designed to spark your discussion, whether you're at a lunchtime meeting with a friend from work or school, on a relationship-building date with your spouse, or at a meeting in your home with your small group.

As we look at the relationship principles of Jesus over these next forty days, our purpose is not to somehow polish our relationship skills to perfection within the pages of this book — an obviously impossible task! Instead, my hope and prayer is that we'll be encouraged to set off in a new direction — the direction of relating to others the way Jesus did. To be sure, it's a journey that takes a lifetime — and then some. But every step will show its worth in our everyday lives.

Place the Highest Value on Relationships

Jesus answered [the teacher of the law], "The most important command is this: 'Listen, people of Israel! The Lord our God is the only Lord. Love the Lord your God with all your heart, all your soul, all your mind, and all your strength.' The second command is this: 'Love your neighbor as you love yourself.' There are no commands more important than these."

Mark 12:29–31 NCV

1

Nothing Is More Important Than Relationships

Relationships are painful. Relationships are wonderful. We all live in the drama that plays out between these two truths.

I think of Neal and Robin when I think of the drama of relationships. Married for only a few years, their life together had started strong. And then, with a suddenness that tore their world apart, Robin suffered a brain hemorrhage. As I sat with Neal in the waiting room on the night it happened, we heard the doctor speak in hushed tones about high-risk surgery and low odds of success. Even if Robin were to survive the surgery, she would likely be in a semiconscious state for the rest of her life. Neal's immediate response was simple faith and sacrificial love. He believed that God had a plan even in this dire circumstance, and Neal was committed to love Robin, no matter what it would take.

Robin survived the surgery, and Neal kept his commitment to love. Day after day, he sat with Robin and spoke to her and nurtured her. Little by little, he loved her to unexpected restoration. Robin learned to speak haltingly and began to be able to use her hands and arms again. She has even taken a few victorious steps on her own. Almost every weekend at church, there they are—Neal, a shining example of overcoming love, and Robin, a powerful example of overwhelming courage and faith. Robin sometimes wonders just what she can accomplish for God in a wheelchair. The truth is, she speaks a life-changing sermon on the power of love by her mere presence. Those who have been involved in Robin's care see her life as a miracle. The greatest miracle, they say, isn't in the healing (they've seen bodies healed before) but in the love. This is the love of a couple who made the choice to continue to love, even in the most crushing of circumstances—Neal having chosen to practice sacrificial love in a marriage that wasn't close to what he and Robin had dreamed it would be, and Robin having chosen to accept and return Neal's love rather than allowing her own hurt to push him away.

> *Relationships are painful. Relationships are wonderful. We all live in the drama that plays out between these two truths.*

Relationships are filled with both wonder and pain. When I think of the pain of relationships, literally hundreds of pictures flood into my mind from my thirty years as a pastor:

- a couple on the verge of a divorce neither one wants yet both are choosing
- parents who can't get through to their child, no matter how much time, money, and heartache they invest
- a son whose dad has treated him with the cruel contempt of abuse

- a friend whose feeling of betrayal is so deep that she never wants to trust anyone again

When I consider the wonder of relationships, I am equally overwhelmed:

- a marriage no one thought could be restored—but it was
- friendships in a small group that have become the bedrock of life
- a family that would surely fall apart when the pressure of an illness hit—and yet they all came together in the most amazing way

When Jesus came to this earth, he demonstrated that he understands both the wonder and the pain of your relationships. He experienced them both. He came to begin a new relationship with you—a relationship that will strengthen all your relationships. Jesus came to show you how to enjoy a new way of relating to God and to others. For these next forty days, we're going to focus on what Jesus did and what Jesus taught about relationships. Each week, we will focus on one of six basic relationship principles of Jesus.

Where Do We Begin?

We begin our journey with Jesus' teaching about priorities. Here's the truth Jesus taught us: *Nothing is more important than relationships.*

I don't remember the time or the place or the conference, but the question the moderator asked has stuck in my mind. What I recall most vividly is the answer that immediately flashed into my thoughts.

Here is the question:

Suppose you're in a rubber life raft with a friend. You're approaching an island. The raft is leaking, and you are within sight of land. In the raft with you are a set of signal flares, a week's supply of canned food, and a five gallon container of water. You must throw one of these items overboard if you're going to make it to the island. Which one do you choose?

I have to admit, the first answer that hit me was "the friend."

Now don't sit there with a pious "I've never thought anything like that" look! This silly thought that leaped into my mind was a reminder of how easy it is to value things over people. And who among us hasn't struggled with that feeling?

Priorities become most important when we must make choices. If we had enough time to do everything, everything could be a priority. *But we don't* have enough time to do everything. If we had the power to do every good thing we wanted to do, our choices wouldn't be so important. *But we can't* do every good thing we want to do.

When Jesus spoke about the priority of relationships, he could not have been clearer. He taught that relationships must be given the highest of values — and thankfully he also taught us *how* to give our relationships the highest value.

Experience the Truth

Throughout this book, we will come back again and again to experiences from the life of Jesus. I encourage you to allow these stories from the Gospels to draw you in! These relationship events from Jesus' life provide an opportunity to learn from *the* relationship expert. Consider what it would have been like to be an eyewitness to the things Jesus taught and did. As you read this experience from the life of Jesus, put yourself there in the crowd with Jesus on that day long ago.

EXPERIENCE THE TRUTH

One of the most noticeable things about Jesus' interactions with others is how people loved to ask him questions. Crowds press in with questions; Jesus' disciples call him aside for questions; and those who disagree with Jesus try to trap him with questions. It's easy to dislike this third group, and it often seems as though Jesus is wasting his time when talking with them. Doesn't he know that their questions are just thinly veiled attempts to trick him into saying something they can use to accuse him? Yet he patiently listens to their questions, and he answers them one by one.

This day the questions are coming fast and furious. One group asks a question about paying taxes; another group launches into a series of questions about marriage. Jesus' answers are brilliant and right to the heart, as always, but it seems that maybe it's time to move on and talk to some who are more open to what he has to say. Then a teacher from the edge of the crowd asks a question with a slightly different tone. There seems to be a genuineness to his question not heard from the others. He simply asks, "Of all the commandments, which is the most important?"

In Jesus' answer is the most important statement about relationships you'll ever hear. As Jesus speaks, he leaves no doubt as to the value he places on relationships:

"The most important [commandment] ... is this: ... 'Love the Lord your God with all your heart and with all your soul and with all your mind and with all your strength.' The second is this: 'Love your neighbor as yourself.'"

Based on Mark 12:28-34

Jesus' simple, clear answer to this question has the power to take our breath away. By choosing these two commands as the most important of all of the Old Testament commands, Jesus tells us how deeply he values relationships. He values our relationship with God, and he values our relationships with each other. Lesson one in Jesus' teaching about relationships is simply this: *Nothing is more important than relationships!*

From beginning to end, nothing is more important than relationships. In the beginning, God created you for relationships. He made you to relate to him and to others. Miss out on relationships, and you're missing the core reason for which God put you on this planet. And in the end, nothing is more important, because nothing will last longer than relationships. Your relationships with God and others will last all the way into eternity. Jesus knows full well that the swirling wonder and pain of our relationships tempt us to move them down our priority list. "Who needs this?" we say, and so reduce our lives to simple hobbies, tasks, and entertainments. That's not the answer! When I try to make less important that which is truly *most* important, it only causes more confusion. A life without relationships may well be a simpler life, but it is also an empty life. The path to the greatest life possible and the greatest joy possible is found in the priority that Jesus taught us to keep at the top of the list: *Place the highest value on relationships.*

DAY ONE
Thinking about My Relationships

Point to Ponder: Place the highest value on relationships.

Verse to Remember: *"The most important [commandment]," answered Jesus, "is this: ... 'Love the Lord your God with all your heart and with all your soul and with all your mind and with all your strength.' The second is this: 'Love your neighbor as yourself'"* (Mark 12:29–31).

Question to Consider: Have I asked Jesus if what I'm doing is what's most important?

Tomorrow: The attraction of lesser things

2

The Attraction
of Lesser Things

Place the highest value on relationships! Not on money, but
on relationships—first with God and then with others. Not
on time, but on relationships—first with God and then
with others. Not on things, but on relationships—first
with God and then with others. Not on your work, but on
relationships—first with God and then with others.

"Yeah, yeah, I know that," you may be thinking. Of course
you do. We all *know* this. The problem we have with valuing
relationships is not in the knowing but in the doing.

Think for a moment about how easy it is for the
unimportant to intrude on the truly important in our
relationships:

- You get up early to spend a few minutes with God to
  start the day, but you end up reading stock quotes or
  sports scores instead.
- Your best friend is pouring out her heart to you, but

you're distracted by that little piece of spinach stuck in her teeth.

- Your spouse is talking about something really important, and your mind keeps wandering to the fact that your favorite TV show started two minutes ago.
- Your child is actually talking to you for once, yet you are so pressured by the tasks of the day that you find yourself rushing the conversation.
- You're writing a chapter on the importance of relationships, yet when your wife interrupts to discuss something important to her heart, your first response is to feel irritated. (Oh, sorry, this last one may have been more for me than for you!)

We could discuss dozens upon dozens of reasons why we give relationships a lesser priority. In the end, understanding why we do it is not nearly as important as changing the fact that we do it so regularly. This is one of those issues where just understanding why has little power to bring about change. Sometimes the answer to a problem comes through personal reflection alone—but this isn't one of those times. We're talking about relationships—and so it only makes sense that you have to get outside of yourself for your relationships to change. You'll never change your relational priorities by continually doing an internal examination of your priorities. The only way to change your priorities is to begin to *make different choices* in your relationships.

Jesus teaches us how to make different choices. What he teaches takes just two sentences to say but a lifetime to put into practice: *Love God with all your heart, soul, mind, and strength. Love your neighbor as yourself.* That's it! Jesus

teaches that we must replace our old set of values with a
new set—and we must then begin to *act* on this new set of
values. First we renew our priorities, and then we act on those
renewed priorities. When Jesus taught that love for God and
love for our neighbor are to come first, he showed us which
values are to have first priority in our lives. Then he described
how to live out the priority of loving God in the words "with
all your heart and with all your soul and with all your mind
and with all your strength" and the priority of loving others
in the words "as yourself." During the next several days, we'll
explore some ideas for putting these words into practice. But
first let's review what Jesus said was *not* important when
compared to the things that are of first importance.

There is a difference between what we think we should
value and what we truly value. Take thirty seconds to ask
yourself what it is you actually place value on. Here are five
questions to jump-start your thoughts in an honest direction:

- What's the first thing you think about in the morning?
- What does your schedule tell you about your priorities?
- As you look at your checkbook, what gets paid, no matter
  what?
- What do you find yourself talking about most?
- What's the last thing you think about when your head
  hits the pillow at night?

We've already looked at Jesus' clear statements that
loving God should be the most important pursuit in life and
that loving others should be a close second. He also spoke
about the need to avoid pursuing the lesser values that can
get in the way of relationships. Let's look at two of the most

intrusive of these lesser values—money and tasks. Don't get me wrong. There's nothing inherently wrong with making money or with accomplishing tasks. We're not talking about whether these are good or bad; we're focused on the issue of *priorities.*

Relationships Are More Important Than Money

Jesus talked about money and relationships in his most famous sermon—the Sermon on the Mount.

> "No one can serve two masters. For you will hate one and love the other, or be devoted to one and despise the other. You cannot serve both God and money.
>
> "So I tell you, don't worry about everyday life—whether you have enough food, drink, and clothes. Doesn't life consist of more than food and clothing? Look at the birds. They don't need to plant or harvest or put food in barns because your heavenly Father feeds them. And you are far more valuable to him than they are. Can all your worries add a single moment to your life? Of course not.
>
> "And why worry about your clothes? Look at the lilies and how they grow. They don't work or make their clothing, yet Solomon in all his glory was not dressed as beautifully as they are. And if God cares so wonderfully for flowers that are here today and gone tomorrow, won't he more surely care for you? You have so little faith!
>
> "So don't worry about having enough food or drink or clothing. Why be like the pagans who are so deeply concerned about these things? Your heavenly Father already knows all your needs, and he will give you all

you need from day to day if you live for him and make the Kingdom of God your primary concern."

Matthew 6:24-33 NLT

As we consider our priorities, three relational truths from this passage are vital. First, notice that Jesus said we "cannot serve both God and money." He didn't say "should not" or "might not want to attempt to"; he said "*cannot.*" Jesus teaches us that competing values cannot coexist. One will overwhelm the other.

Our modern-day answer is, "I'll manage my life better, and then I'll be able to do more! I'll find time for being completely committed to God *and* for making money — and for recreation and career and hobbies too!" Jesus says, "You cannot serve both God and money," and we think, "Well, Jesus obviously didn't understand how to multitask!" It doesn't matter how well you manage your life or how many labor-saving, time-saving devices you buy; if you try to hold on to competing values, one will always overwhelm the other.

And here's the strange thing: the lesser value almost always overwhelms the greater. Lesser values take less faith *and* less effort. The lesser value seems easier, and so it will constantly draw you in. Because

> If you try to hold on to competing values, one will always overwhelm the other.

to all appearances you can reach a lesser value more quickly, you'll be continually tempted to make it your first priority. Those who try to love both God and money end up loving just money.

Lesser values don't deliver on their promise. That's what

makes them lesser! A while back, I received an email from my friend Bucky. He was on the cusp of a career change, with all of the energy, anxiety, and evaluation such a change creates for anyone. His son had asked him to spend college spring break driving around the old South, visiting all the places where "Dad grew up." In the email, Bucky said, "I really can't afford to be gone right now but decided that twenty years from now, no one will remember that I took time away from my new work, but my son will (hopefully) remember it for the rest of his life. Pray for our safety, and that I will be able to resist the temptation to do emails and make phone calls every night!" That's a choice for the greater value of relationships — a choice for what will last.

There is a second truth here, found in Jesus' question, "Doesn't life consist of more than food and clothing?" The answer is, "Of course it does!" The striking thing about the lesser values is that the more of them you achieve, the more you realize how little power they have to bring fulfillment. You end up lying awake in the middle of the night with these very words of Jesus running through your mind: "Doesn't life consist of more ...?"

If you're looking for an adventure, you'll find it in having the faith to put your relationships first.

Revolutionary War hero Patrick Henry is famous for knowing something about values. His stirring cry "Give me liberty or give me death" is certainly a values statement — trumpeting his commitment to the value of freedom. He also had something to say about the value of a relationship with God over lesser things. Near the end of his life, he penned these words: "I have now disposed of all my property to my family. There is one thing more I wish I could give them, and that is the Christian religion. If they had that and I had not given them one shilling, they would be rich; and if they had not that, and I had given them all the world, they would be poor."*

There is a third truth in Matthew 6 that has the power to refocus our lives. Jesus says to those he was teaching, "You have so little faith!" The question Jesus posed that prompted this exclamation was, "If God cares so wonderfully for flowers that are here today and gone tomorrow, won't he more surely care for you?" When you boil it all down, questions about priority are questions about faith. If I have faith that God will care for me, it frees me to live with a certain set of priorities; if instead I feel that it's up to me to take care of myself, my priorities will go in a completely different direction.

In order to make your relationship with God and others the top priority, you're going to have to trust God like never before! If you're looking for a challenge, if you're looking for an adventure, you'll find it in having the faith to put your relationships first.

Relationships Are More Important Than Tasks

Not only are relationships more important than money; they are also more important than tasks. Jesus' life is filled with encounters that show how he balanced the needs of people and the tasks before him:

---

*Quoted in C. C. Bombaugh, *Facts and Fancies for the Curious from the Harvest-Fields of Literature* (Whitefish, Mont.: Kessinger, 2003), 622.

- While being pressured to hurry through the crowds to see Jairus's daughter, who was near death, Jesus stops to give a shy woman the opportunity to voice her faith (see Mark 5:21–43).
- When the disciples tell some parents that Jesus' schedule won't allow time for their children to be in his presence, Jesus says, "Let the little children come to me, and do not hinder them" (Mark 10:14).
- Jesus and his disciples plan to get away from the crowd, only to have five thousand men meet them at their place of quiet retreat. As the day gets late, the disciples show Jesus the logic of sending the people away to buy something to eat. But Jesus says, "You give them something to eat" (Mark 6:37).
- Jesus' disciples are shocked to find him taking the time to talk to a woman beside a well in Samaria (see John 4), because other teachers in Jesus' day thought themselves too important to speak to women in public.

I could go on and on and on.

It's tempting to think, "Of course Jesus had time for people. Things weren't as fast-paced in his culture as in ours." The truth is, whenever tasks need to be accomplished, there is the temptation to make the task you are doing more important than the people for whom you are doing the task. Did you notice that in every example above there was someone who wanted to hurry Jesus on to the next important item on his schedule? And in every case Jesus chose meeting a person's need above following his schedule of tasks for that day.

I tend to value time and tasks. Getting things done can be very important to me. As a young pastor, I devoured books about how to get more done in less time. God used one of those books to get my attention in the area of relationships. I'm sure you've noted that God has a wonderful sense of humor—and one of the ways I've seen it is in how he will use the most unexpected means to get a message across. If you're tempted to doubt God's humor, let me remind you that when the prophet Balaam tried to distance himself from God, God used his donkey to speak to him (see Numbers 22:28)! If God could speak to Balaam through his donkey, he could certainly speak to me about relationships through a book on time management. As I searched the book for the next tidbit on how to get more done, two sentences jumped out and struck my heart like lightning:

> God does not demand of me that I accomplish great things. He does demand of me that I strive for excellence in my relationships.*

Wow! I remember these words because I copied them onto a three-by-five card and taped the card to the inside of my briefcase. For years and years, until the card became yellowed with age and curled at the edges, it was the first thing I saw when I opened my case to "get to work."

It was a statement that put the fear of God in me. When I first read it, I realized how easy it would be to miss God's priorities for my life. I deeply wanted to do God's will, but "God's will" was often defined as "build a bigger church, be in a more significant ministry, accomplish greater tasks." These two sentences reminded me that it would be the easiest thing

---

*Ted W. Engstrom, *The Making of a Christian Leader* (Grand Rapids: Zondervan, 1976), 81.

in the world to chase after accomplishments my entire life and yet be left with mediocre relationships.

I don't want you to misunderstand what I'm saying. There is nothing wrong with serving in a big, visible ministry. And there is nothing wrong with serving with all you have in what others (not God) might see as a small, hidden ministry. There is certainly nothing wrong with wanting to do great things for God — and accomplishing great things for him. The problem is that it's just too easy to start doing the great things for yourself and not for him. It can happen in the blink of an eye. Service is then replaced with selfishness. We all struggle with selfishness, so how do we protect ourselves from letting our ego take center stage? That's where the priority of relationships comes in! A healthy relationship with God and healthy relationships with others have the power to keep our commitments to the things and the tasks in our lives from getting out of balance.

Thinking about My Relationships

Point to Ponder: God does not demand of me that I accomplish great things. He does demand of me that I strive for excellence in my relationships.

Verse to Remember: *"So I tell you, don't worry about everyday life — whether you have enough food, drink, and clothes. Doesn't life consist of more than food and clothing?"* (Matthew 6:25 NLT).

Question to Consider: What do the ways in which I spend my time and money say about the top priorities in my life?

Tomorrow: Love God with all your heart

Love God
with All Your Heart

Let's get practical. It's easy to *talk* about the importance of relationships. But how can we turn that talk into action? How do we *do* relationships? We need some places where we can plug in and get started.

The powerful statements in the Bible can easily feel like a high-voltage electrical line. You can see and feel the power in the statements, but you're just not quite sure how to plug in. It's hard to envision how something that high-powered could fit into your daily life! Because most of us know we need to do these things, it can be frustrating to even talk about them. It's just a reminder of what we're not doing. Who wants to be reminded of a diet when you're in the middle of eating a hot fudge sundae? The good news is this: the Bible also shows us how to plug in, where to get started, and what to do. For the next five days, we're going to reflect on what Jesus' great commandment has to say about where we begin.

Before we dive into these truths, let me say something that might shock you: God's principles don't change our lives.

What? How can I as a teacher of the Bible say that? I'll admit I'm playing with words to get your attention—because I don't want you to miss this: It is your *faith* in God's principles that changes your life! This statement is not meant to give any of us the credit, because it's *God* who gives us the power to have faith. Instead, it's a reminder that knowing more facts and ideas and principles—even if they're God's principles—does not have the power to change your relationships. The power to change starts with faith—with trusting God—and then acting on that faith.

I invite you to make your journey through these next pages a faith exercise. If you don't like the word *exercise*, you can call it a faith adventure. Whatever you decide to call it, choose to walk with Jesus through a process of faith that has the power to transform every relationship.

One word from Jesus' words about loving God echoes loudly again and again. *All.* *All* your heart. *All* your soul. *All* your mind. *All* your strength.

Love him with all your heart. Your heart is where you feel. I'm choosing to focus here on the emotional side of the broader idea of "heart" in the Bible. And it needs focus, because our expressions of love to God often have a formality that can quench our faith. Our Father wants his children to express their feelings of love for him!

Love him with all your soul. Your soul is where you decide. Have you ever decided to do something, even though you didn't feel like doing it? What caused you to be able to do so? You have a will. You're not driven by your emotions or even by your thoughts. Your soul decides. It can decide not to decide—to allow your emotions to have free reign; but even doing that is a decision of your soul.

Love him with all your mind. Your mind is where you think. Your mind is where thoughts, impressions, intelligence, and learning happen. Faith in God doesn't mean we stop thinking. Just the opposite, in fact: God wants us to love him with our minds.

Love him with all your strength. Your strength is where you physically interact with the world around you. At some point, a heart, soul, and mind of love must be translated into real actions in a real world. It takes energy; it takes strength.

Heart, soul, mind, strength. Feelings, decisions, thoughts, actions. If you want to change the way you relate to God, your plan must involve these four. If you're not feeling something about your way of relating to God, deciding something about it, thinking something about it, and doing something about it—then you won't see any change.

So how do you plug in? How do you love God with your heart, soul, mind, and strength? Without practical action steps, these commitments will remain only ideas that never make their way into your everyday life. For today and the next two days, we'll focus on one practical thing you can do in each of these four areas.

> The power to change starts with faith—with trusting God—and then acting on that faith.

If you're like me, this is the part of a book you tend to skip. I say to myself, "OK, I've got the concept down—now I'll skate on to the next chapter." Our object is not "getting new concepts." You can read a philosophy text if that's what you're looking for. Our goal is relationships that are transformed by the example and power of Jesus Christ. And in order for this goal to begin to be realized, we have to choose to *do something different* in our lives because of the example and power of Jesus' life. Will you choose to act in new ways this week? If you do, you will begin to see your relationships truly change.

Here's a practical place to get started in this adventure of loving God with all your heart: *Talk to God out loud and with emotion.*

Study the psalms. God called David, the writer of many of the psalms, "a man after his own heart" (1 Samuel 13:14; Acts 13:22). David's prayers in the psalms contain a gold mine of wisdom about loving God with all your heart. As you read the Old Testament book of Psalms, it is clear that David's prayers had more emotion than most of our prayers do. In fact, you may well find more emotion in one sentence of David's prayers than in an entire year of many Christians' daily devotions.

Most of our private prayers are silent; we "speak" them in our minds. There is nothing wrong with praying in this way; in fact you should. However, it can lead easily to prayers that are more about our thoughts than our heart. To really put your heart into something you need to say it aloud. I didn't say *loud,* just *out loud.* Try talking to God at the same volume you'd use in talking to your friend if you were having a conversation in the car.

> Our goal is relationships that are transformed by the example and power of Jesus Christ.

And as you talk to him, tell him your feelings. You see the same pattern again and again in David's psalms. He's facing a huge problem, and he begins to pour out his heart. He talks to God with emotion about the problem. And before he comes to the end of the psalm, his heart is at peace. The problems are still there, but David's heart has been refocused in the course of the twenty or thirty verses of the psalm.

David's heart is settled in twenty or thirty verses, yet some of us live with unsettled hearts on an issue for twenty or thirty *years!* Without oversimplifying the depth of hurt that our hearts can experience, I have no doubt that one of the reasons for this lack of peace is that we never share our emotions with God. We pray logically. We pray consistently. We even pray biblically. But we don't follow David's example of praying emotionally.

How do you pray more emotionally? Here are seven things you can do, with a prayer of David as an example under each:

1. Talk to God about your feelings.

> *I am worn out from groaning;*
> *all night long I flood my bed with weeping*
> *and drench my couch with tears.*
>
> Psalm 6:6

2. Talk to God about your weaknesses.

> *Turn to me, LORD, and be merciful to me,*
> *because I am lonely and weak.*
>
> Psalm 25:16 TEV

3. Talk to God about his strengths.

> *Who is this King of glory?*
> *The LORD strong and mighty,*
> *the LORD mighty in battle.*
>
> Psalm 24:8

4. Tell God your fears.

> *Fear and trembling overwhelm me.*
> *I can't stop shaking.*
>
> Psalm 55:5 NLT

5. Pour out to God the desires of your heart.

> *You, Lord, know every one*
>   *of my deepest desires,*
> *and my noisy groans*
>   *are no secret to you.*
>
> Psalm 38:9 CEV

6. Openly and emotionally admit your sins to God.

> *I am on the verge of collapse,*
>   *facing constant pain.*
> *But I confess my sins;*
>   *I am deeply sorry for what I have done.*
>
> Psalm 38:17–18 NLT

7. Say out loud what you know to be true.

> *[David] sang this song to the LORD on the day the LORD rescued him from all his enemies and from Saul.*

> *I love you, LORD; you are my strength.*
> *The LORD is my rock, my fortress, and my savior;*
>   *my God is my rock, in whom I find protection.*
> *He is my shield, the strength of my salvation,*
>   *and my stronghold.*
>
> Psalm 18:1–2 NLT

Act on this right now. Say to God, "Father, here is what is *really* hurting me right now!" Or, "Here is what I *feel* about this problem I'm facing." Or, "Here is what I *love* about your character." Love God with *all* your heart.

Thinking about My Relationships

Point to Ponder: The path to putting God first starts with the word *all.*

Verse to Remember: *"Seek first [God's] kingdom and his righteousness, and all these things will be given to you as well"* (Matthew 6:33).

Question to Consider: Do I tell God what I feel, or do I tell him what I think he wants to hear?

Tomorrow: Love God with all your soul

Love God
with All Your Soul

Yesterday we began looking at the importance of the word *all* in making a relationship with God your first priority and at loving God with *all your heart*. Now we turn to *all your soul*.

If I ask, "Where is your heart?" you point to your chest. "Where is your mind?" That's easy. But where is your soul? We don't even know where to point. What is your soul?

A study of the Old and New Testament words for *soul* gives a glimpse at what Jesus means when he says, "Love God with all your soul." The Old Testament uses the Hebrew word *nephesh*, which means "to breathe." Behind this word is the idea that God breathes life into us. You're a living soul. You have an awareness held by nothing else in creation because God himself breathes life into you. The New Testament uses the Greek word *psychē*, which lies at the root of our word *psychology*. It has to do with your will, your drive, the passion of your life, the power by which you live. Put these Old and New Testament words together, and you get a fairly good idea of what the soul is. Your soul is your desires and passions.

Your soul is your God-given personality. Your soul is your will to decide; it has to do with the direction your life is taking. At the essence, your soul is your LIFE—life in capital letters because we're talking about the kind of life that only God can give—the Creator life. Your soul is the passion with which you're living, the personality you've been given, the path your life is taking, the power in your being.

To Love God with All Your Soul, Seek Him Passionately

Most of us sense in our gut that having some kind of relationship with God must be part of what makes up a healthy soul. Because our soul is the expression of our life passion, a relationally healthy soul will passionately seek to express love for God.

Jesus told many stories about this kind of passion, this kind of thirst, in our lives. Many of these stories about the passion with which we seek God and his kingdom had to do with finding something that was lost. Jesus told of a woman who had lost a silver coin and searched with all the passion she had to find it. He told of a shepherd who had lost one sheep and left his ninety-nine other sheep to go after that one sheep with all his passion and energy. Jesus told of a father who had lost a son and passionately celebrated when the prodigal returned (see Luke 15).

> A relationally healthy soul will passionately seek to express love for God.

You've had the experience of losing something that was important to you. Maybe it was your keys, some money, or a report due for school or work. You turned the house upside down to find it. "I must find it! I won't stop until I find it." That's passion. That's the way to seek God. Seek him passionately—with *all your soul.*

To Love God with All Your Soul, Love Him Personally

You are like nothing else and no one else. You're the only one in all of creation who can love the Lord like you can. You're the only *you* in all of creation. When you love the Lord, you love him with a unique voice—a voice different in tone, different in soul, from any other voice God hears in all of creation. Love God uniquely with the personality he's fashioned into your life.

Your soul can be injured if you think that true love for God means we all must worship in the same way. If I see somebody raising their hands to love the Lord, I think I have to do that because "that's what you do to love the Lord." If they're raising one hand, I'm raising one hand; right hand, left hand, left foot—whatever they do, I do. But we need to learn from others how to love without feeling we must copy their exact actions or adopt their personality. We tend to think, "I don't want to stand out too much in the way I love God; I'd rather just blend in." If you really love him with your God-given personality, the way you express your love will be a bit different from everybody else. Not strange—different. It's going to be wonderfully different.

To Love God with All Your Soul, Decide to Do What He Wants You to Do

One moment stands above all others in history as the greatest example of loving God with all one's soul. It took place on the night before Jesus died, as he talked to his Father in the garden of Gethsemane. Knowing that the next day he would face the physical, emotional, and spiritual torture of the cross, Jesus prayed, "Not my will, but yours be done" (Luke 22:42). Jesus set aside anything he may have desired and determined to do only what the Father directed.

How do you set your soul to make such a radical decision? Jesus shows the way. You set the direction of your soul by talking to God. The power to follow Jesus' example is found in being able to pray the prayer that Jesus prayed: "Not my will, Lord, but yours be done."

The movie *Amazing Grace* tells the story of the passion of William Wilberforce to abolish the slave trade in England. This movie does not shrink from picturing how the soul of Wilberforce was informed and inspired by his faith in Jesus Christ. At one point, the camera pans across the table at Wilberforce's bedside and shows the book he has been reading — *The Rise and Progress of Religion in the Soul* by Philip Doddridge. Philip Doddridge was one of the great spiritual influences of the seventeenth and eighteenth centuries, primarily because he knew how to set his soul by talking to God. The students at the school

> *The power to follow Jesus' example is found in being able to pray the prayer that Jesus prayed: "Not my will, Lord, but yours be done."*

for ministry he established appreciated his lectures and, according to some, endured his sermons. But it was his prayers that most influenced their lives. These students felt in his prayers a sincerity and understanding of the human heart that went straight to their souls. Doddridge pens this prayer expressing the soul behind the commitment "not my will, but yours be done":

> This day do I, with the utmost solemnity, surrender myself to thee. I renounce all former lords that have had dominion over me; and I consecrate to thee all that I am, and all that I have; the faculties of my mind, the members of my body, my worldly possessions, my time, and my influence over others; to be all used entirely for thy glory, and resolutely employed in obedience to thy commands, as long as thou continuest me in life.... To thee I leave the management of all events, and say without reserve, "Not my will, but thine be done."*

As a result of this kind of soul, this book became one of the most printed, read, and translated books of his day and well beyond. Wilberforce was encouraged to read the book by a friend while on holiday in France. He later counted it as one of his greatest influences toward faith in Christ. Doddridge did not have physical strength; he suffered from weakness and illness for most of his life. He didn't have an easy life. He was the twentieth child born into a family in which eighteen of his siblings died as babies or young children. His mother died when he was eight, his father when he was thirteen, and he

---

*Philip Doddridge, *The Rise and Progress of Religion in the Soul* (Andover, Mass.: Flagg and Gould, printers, 1831), 162.

then suffered as a result of the mismanagement of funds by his guardian. Yet focusing his soul on God's will caused him to influence others in ways that can still be measured today.[*]

If you've been a believer for any length of time, you've discovered that it can easily become your habit to try to love God with *part* but not all of your soul. You pray, "Your will be done, Lord, not my will," in your church life but not your business life, or in your family life but not your personal thought life. This week, stamp *all* of your life with the prayer, "Not my will, Lord, but yours be done." Even if you feel, "I don't know if I can honestly pray this prayer for every area," go ahead and begin with the prayer, "God, I want your will, but I want my will also. I know it's wrong, but it's how I feel. So I ask you to work in my heart to get me to the place where I can pray, 'Not my will, but your will be done.' I want to learn to love you with all my soul."

---

[*]See David Lyle Jeffrey, ed., *English Spirituality in the Age of Wesley* (Vancouver, B.C.: Regent College Publishing, 2000), 174–76; G. Ella, "Philip Doddridge," *The Banner of Sovereign Grace Truth* 6, no. 7 (September 1998).

Thinking about My Relationships

Point to Ponder: When you love the Lord, you love him with a unique voice—a voice that is different in soul from any other voice God hears in all of creation.

Verse to Remember: *"Blessed are those who hunger and thirst for righteousness, for they will be filled"* (Matthew 5:6).

Question to Consider: Where do I need to pray, "Lord, your will be done," in order to love God with all my soul?

Tomorrow: Love God with all your mind and strength

5

Love God
with All Your Mind
and Strength

Stop for a moment and totally clear your mind. What was
your first thought after you cleared your mind? It may be
worship. Or it may be worry. It may be something that
happened at work today. It may be a negative thought. A
selfish thought. Not all of our thoughts are pure thoughts.
Not all of our thoughts are thoughts about God.

With All Your Mind

How do you love the Lord your God with all your mind? It
obviously has to do with the thoughts that run through your
mind throughout the day. At its most basic, to love God with
all your mind is to know that God's thoughts are thoughts
of love toward you and to decide that your thoughts will be
thoughts of love toward God.

Turning your thoughts toward God is easy to understand

but difficult to do. There is so much to worry or distract or tempt you. If you've ever tried to turn your thoughts toward God and ended up with worried or wasted thoughts instead, you understand the frustration. Where do you get started? What can you do to make a difference in the way you think?

To love God with all your mind, you must put God's words into your mind. If your mind is filled with only your thoughts or the thoughts imposed on you by others, of course you'll be frustrated when trying to have worshipful thoughts. Left to itself, your mind will drift toward anxious or selfish thoughts. The truth of God's Word has the power to change the channel of your thinking.

One of the most powerful verses in the Bible for turning your thoughts to God is Philippians 4:8. I urge you to memorize this verse:

> Finally, brothers, whatever is true, whatever is noble, whatever is right, whatever is pure, whatever is lovely, whatever is admirable—if anything is excellent or praiseworthy—think about such things.

By memorizing this verse, you'll be able to bring it to mind each time you face a circumstance that tempts you to turn your thoughts from love for God. I first memorized this verse as a teenager, and I've brought it to mind literally thousands upon thousands of times in my thirty-five years as a believer in Jesus. As the temptation to focus on some selfishness, lust, or pride came, I'd recall this verse in my mind. My guess is that I'm not the only one whose thoughts turn so easily from God to the worries and wants of this world.

The command in Philippians 4:8 to "think about such

things" is a reminder of an obvious but all-important truth: God holds us responsible for what we think. I can make choices about what I think that literally change the direction of my life. The verb tense here indicates a *continual* habit of thought. I make this kind of thinking a part of my day. In the eight specific virtues Paul urges us to think about here, we can easily draft a blueprint of the direction in which our minds are to think. Let's spend a few moments reflecting on these virtues, and as we do, I encourage you to turn your thoughts in the direction this verse points you to go.

> The truth of God's Word has the power to change the channel of your thinking.

"Whatever is true": Meditate on God's truth. The Greek word translated "true" (*alēthēs*) refers to things that won't let you down, things you can depend on in life. When you focus on things that won't let you down, your anxiety level goes down. The love of God won't let you down. The truth of God, revealed in the Bible, will not let you down.

"Whatever is noble": Appreciate God's worth. The idea behind the word *noble* is that of a person who is aware of the fact that God is at work all around him or her. You are aware of what God is doing in the world, and so your eyes are lifted from the common things around you to focus on the godly.

"Whatever is right": Cooperate with God's plan. "Right" things have to do with God's directions, God's will. Before you can do the right thing, you have to think the right thing.

"Whatever is pure": Appropriate God's cleansing. When you pray, "God, cleanse my mind of sin," can you take away the memory of the fact that you've sinned? No, you can't. Even now, the memory of a sin may intrude—and the memory brings guilt. You can't erase a memory or replace a memory, but you can refocus your thoughts on whatever is pure. Right now, refocus your thoughts by thinking about the cross of Jesus—about the sacrifice he made there to offer you the gift of forgiveness.

"Whatever is lovely": Anticipate God's abundance. The word *lovely* means not so much "pretty" as "enjoyable." We all love to enjoy things, to be entertained. To think about whatever is lovely is to let God entertain you. This may sound strange, because entertainment means sporting events, movies, television, plays, and concerts. But couldn't the greatness, the abundance, the gifts of God entertain you in a different way—in fact, in a much greater way? I'm using the word *entertain* not in the lowest sense of the word but in the highest—the sense of deeply enjoying something. If you can't enjoy God with your mind, you're never going to love him with all your mind. We often fail to realize this truth. Whatever you're doing—whether with your family or on vacation or at work—enjoy the abundance and the goodness of God. When looking at a blue sky or at the clouds drifting across, take a moment to be entertained by the creativity of God. Enjoy who he really is.

"Whatever is admirable": Communicate God's encouragement. The word used here has behind it the idea of something you admire in others that is worth talking about. If you're going to love God with your thoughts, you have to love the people he made in that same way. It's all too easy to see the faults in others. Loving God with all your mind involves looking for what's best in others and telling them, "I see something of God's character in you."

"If anything is excellent": Be motivated by God's greatness. Let your day be driven, moment by moment, by thinking about the greatness of God. There are a lot of motivations that are short-term: selfishness, greed, guilt, fear, worry, pride. Find motivation for your life in God's greatness — the motivation that will last forever.

"If anything is praiseworthy": Celebrate God's goodness. Celebrate in your thoughts what God is doing. The evident goodness of God is all around you. Think about something that is worth celebrating right now.

Let's confront a thought you may be having about the eight ways of thinking listed in this verse. We know God commands us to think this way, but there may be something about this that feels intellectually dishonest. "There is so much evil in the world," we say to ourselves, "and to only think about what is good seems like I'm burying my head in the sand." God isn't telling us to pretend there is no evil. Just the opposite! He is telling us to confront and defeat evil by turning our thoughts to him.

Isaiah 26:3 (LB) pictures the results of turning our thoughts toward God: "He will keep in perfect peace all those who trust in him, whose thoughts turn often to the Lord!" Would you like your life to have a little more peace? God will keep in perfect peace those whose thoughts turn often to him. If you are to help hurting people find peace, you must have that peace in your own heart. You cannot give to someone else what you do not have.

With All Your Strength

Love God with all your heart, all your soul, all your mind. Then tie it all together by loving him with *all your strength*.

Your strength is where your inner thoughts and feelings touch the outer world. It's where you actually do something about your thoughts and feelings. You want to love the Lord, but sometimes it doesn't play itself out in just the way you'd like it to. How do you translate a desire to love God into your everyday life?

To love God with all your strength, there are three truths you must embrace:

- You must have complete confidence that God can do absolutely anything. Jesus said, "I tell you the truth, anyone who has faith in me will do what I have been doing. He will do even greater things than these, because I am going to the Father" (John 14:12).
- You must be completely convinced that you can do absolutely nothing of ultimate and eternal significance without the power of Jesus Christ. Jesus said, "Apart from me you can do nothing" (John 15:5).
- You must trust God to turn your weakness into his strength. As Paul faced the fact of his weakness, he heard God say to him, "My grace is sufficient for you, for my power is made perfect in weakness." And so Paul responded, "Therefore I will boast all the more gladly about my weaknesses, so that Christ's power may rest on me.... For when I am weak, then I am strong" (2 Corinthians 12:9–10).

There is a difference between an honest admission of weakness and a self-focused feeling of inadequacy. I grew up in a home with a father who suffered from schizophrenia. The chaos that resulted taught me at an early age that there were things I wanted to change but had no power to do so. That experience, along with my personality and perspective, has made it all too easy to go down the road of focusing on my own inadequacy. It's a lot easier for me to see what I think God couldn't do through my life than to see what he surely can do.

You must trust God to turn your weakness into his strength.

How do you deal with feelings of inadequacy? You can try to overcome them by doing things that seem big enough to make you feel significant. You can attempt to erase them by pretending the feelings just don't exist. You can seek to escape from them by immersing yourself in some little hobby or selfish pleasure. You can give in to them and go through life believing you truly are insignificant. I can tell you from personal experience that none of these work! Instead, I'm learning to make the choice to accept my feelings of inadequacy as a weakness and to lean on God's strength. I urge you to ask God to help you make choices of faith in spite of feelings of inadequacy. Don't expect, however, that your choices will suddenly make you feel more adequate. I wish I could tell you they will, but it's just not true. I've never been able to feel better about myself by focusing on myself. Instead of focusing on or fighting your inadequacy, choose faith in a God who is more than adequate. Pray something like this: "Father, you know how I'm feeling about myself right now.

I'm tired of pretending I'm strong, so I ask you to use me in my weakness. I trust in your truth: when I am weak, *you* are strong."

DAY FIVE
Thinking about My Relationships

Point to Ponder: To love God with your mind, you must put God's words into your mind.

Verse to Remember: *Finally, brothers, whatever is true, whatever is noble, whatever is right, whatever is pure, whatever is lovely, whatever is admirable—if anything is excellent or praiseworthy—think about such things* (Philippians 4:8).

Questions to Consider: Where have my thoughts been focused lately? When was the last time I asked God to give me the strength to move forward in his power, even though I was feeling weak?

Tomorrow: Love everyone as your neighbor

6

Love Everyone
as Your Neighbor

Jesus' challenge to love God is more than enough to captivate our thoughts—but then he adds the simple command, "Love your neighbor as yourself."

EXPERIENCE THE TRUTH

Jesus is having yet another discussion with a religious lawyer, who asks Jesus a question others had asked—it was a popular question. But he asks only out of a desire to show his own religiosity. He asks questions not for the answers but for showing off his own intelligence.

The man asks Jesus, "How do I inherit eternal life?" The answer Jesus draws from the man is familiar: "Love the Lord your God with all your heart and soul and strength and mind. And love your neighbor as yourself." "You're right," Jesus said to the man. "Do this and you will live."

The crowd possibly looked at the lawyer with a "that's so simple, why are you wasting our time?" gleam in their eyes. The lawyer's embarrassment must have been obvious. He has not come off looking nearly as impressive as he had hoped! Will he quietly walk away, as so many have, shaking his head in amazement at Jesus' wisdom? Not this man! Instead he tries to justify his first question with another question.

You can almost see him, red-faced and flustered, stammering out, "Umm, well then, who is my neighbor?"

What kind of question is that? Isn't it obvious who your neighbor is? Will Jesus even justify this with an answer?

But Jesus does answer. He tells a story—an unforgettable story—about an injured man lying beside the road that goes from Jerusalem to Jericho. The crowd stirs as he tells about a priest and a temple assistant who pass by without stopping to help the injured man. They're too important, too busy, too holy to touch this stranger beside the road. Some in the listening crowd would likely be nodding their heads in agreement. It is how they would have expected these self-important men to act. Then Jesus brings another character into the story—a Samaritan who is walking down the road. The Jewish crowd to whom Jesus was speaking didn't like Samaritans, and Samaritans didn't like Jews either. Historical disputes had turned into cultural divides and personal distrust. For this Jewish crowd, a Samaritan would be the enemy in most of their stories and the punch line to many of their jokes.

Jesus describes the Samaritan's actions: He stops; he bandages the injured man's wounds; he puts the man on his donkey; he takes the stranger to an inn, where he pays for his continuing care.

As Jesus finishes, the unveiling of the unexpected hero of this story must have hushed the crowd. In the silence of that moment, Jesus looks at the lawyer whose question had prompted the story of the good Samaritan. The Lord gently asks him the loving question, "Which of these three is a neighbor?" The way the lawyer answers tells you he's forgotten about impressing the crowd. Now it's just him and Jesus talking. "The one who helped him," he says.

Based on Luke 10:25 – 37

This is a story to capture every fiber of your being. If Jesus' teaching here doesn't change the way you act toward others, I doubt anything will!

Among the many truths taught in this powerful parable, let's focus today and tomorrow on two clear values that have to do with how we love others. This is a parable that (1) pictures the value of loving *everyone* and (2) speaks to the value of loving *someone. Everyone* means there is no one outside the limits of my love; *someone* means I can only practice love toward people I am with right now. Love that speaks in grand terms about loving everyone yet does nothing to meet in practical ways the need of the person who stands in front of it is not true love. Love that meets the needs of people who are close to it and yet looks on those outside its circle with prejudice is not true love either. Tomorrow we'll look at the value of loving one person in practical ways; today we focus on the value of having love for everyone.

The story about the good Samaritan teaches that I cannot limit the extent of my love. Any time I limit the word *neighbor* to some group smaller than *everyone*, I've missed the meaning of Jesus' words. And let's be honest, it's easy to limit our love. The reasons are as obvious today as they were when Jesus first told this story.

We Limit Our Love because of Our Differences

Jesus shocked those who listened to this parable when he made a Samaritan the hero of the story. For Jesus to answer the question, "Who is my neighbor?" with a story about a Samaritan made it clear that there are no limits to our love. Jesus taught elsewhere, "You have heard that it was said, 'Love your neighbor and hate your enemy.' But I tell you: Love your enemies and pray for those who persecute you" (Matthew 5:43–44). When Jesus said *neighbor,* he meant *everyone!* Whichever person or group would be Samaritans for you — Jesus meant them. Even those who would say they are your enemy.

God wants us to depend on him for the power to love.

This seems so simple. Why is it even important to talk about? Because the moment I take it upon myself to limit the extent of my love, I've slipped away from God's kind of love.

I've descended to a merely human kind of love. God's love is an "everyone/everywhere/all the time" kind of love; human love is a "some people/some places/some of the time" kind of love. Some of us are better than others at human love, but none of us are able to express God's kind of love in our own power. That's the point. *God wants us to depend on him* for the power to love. So he challenges us to love in a way we can only accomplish through daily dependence on his power.

We Limit Our Love because of Our Fears

Besides limiting our love because of our differences, we also limit love because of our fears. When Jesus' listeners heard him tell the story of the good Samaritan, they would have immediately picked up on something we easily miss: *it was a great risk* for this Samaritan to care for the stranger lying beside the road.

It was well known in that day that the road to Jericho was frequented by robbers. The road from Jerusalem to Jericho wound down a steep descent through desolate country. The distance was about seventeen miles on a road that descended over three thousand feet. A common practice was to have one robber lie beside the road as though injured, with other robbers hiding nearby. Anyone who stopped long enough to help would find that he had fallen into a trap. It was a genuine risk for the Samaritan to stop and help.

The risk involved caused two men to pass by on the other side. In identifying them as religious men, Jesus was pointing out another fear: if a religious man touched a man covered in blood, he would become ceremonially unclean.

It's always a risk to love. First century or twenty-first century, it's a risk to love. Samaritan or American or Iranian, it's a risk to love. Whether you're on the road to Jericho, Chicago, or Mexico — it's a risk to love. C. S. Lewis has made this profound observation:

> To love at all is to be vulnerable. Love anything, and your heart will certainly be wrung and possibly be broken. If you want to make sure of keeping it intact, you must give your heart to no one, not even to an animal. Wrap it carefully round with hobbies and little luxuries; avoid all entanglements; lock it up safe in the casket or coffin of your selfishness. But in that casket — safe, dark, motionless, airless — it will change. It will not be broken; it will become unbreakable, impenetrable, irredeemable.[*]

You may have experienced deep hurt because you made the choice to love. It would be only natural to tell yourself, "I'm never going to open myself up to that kind of pain again." Of course you feel that way. Who wants to be wounded? Lewis's statement reminds us that there is an even deeper hurt to be found in *not* loving than in taking the risk to love. If you choose not to love, not only will you be hurt, but the people you could have loved will be hurt in ways you may never know.

Take the risk to love! Take the risk, and begin to set aside a prejudice that has kept an entire group or nationality of people outside the bounds of your love. Take the risk, and begin again to love someone whom you've stopped loving or have refused to love. God knows that when we refuse to love,

---

[*]C. S. Lewis, *The Four Loves* (New York: Harcourt Brace Jovanovich, 1960), 169.

Principle #1: Place the Highest Value on Relationships

bitterness and a feeling of emptiness inevitably grow in our hearts. No hurt or misunderstanding or sin that has been brought on you could be worth the greater hurt of refusing to love.

Love is the greatest risk you'll ever take. There are people who will skydive off Yosemite Valley's El Capitan, yet they are afraid to take the risk to love. I know CEOs who wouldn't flinch from a billion dollar deal, yet they are terrified to love. It's a risk to love, but it is the one risk worth taking more than any other. Keep this in mind: the one relationship you can truly count on is your relationship to Jesus Christ. Lean on your relationship to him as you take the risk to love others. Others may disappoint you — but Jesus will never fail you.

Love Someone
as Your Neighbor

There are two life-challenging truths about love reflected
in the story of the good Samaritan. We looked at the first
yesterday: *I cannot limit the extent of my love.* Today we consider
the second truth: *I must limit the expression of my love.*

While we seek to have God's heart of love for everyone,
love is more than an attitude. It must be translated into
practical actions. God can act in love toward all of us, because
he is all-present and all-powerful. We, on the other hand, are
limited human beings whose love can only be expressed to
one person or group in the moment in which we now live.

One of the issues I struggle with is how to have a love for
everyone while at the same time recognizing that I cannot
meet everyone's needs. If I love them but can't meet their
needs, won't I just be left feeling frustrated? Wouldn't it be
easier to decide to do my best at loving a more manageable
group, such as my family and a few close friends?

Jesus is our teacher and our example. He teaches us to
love everyone. In his last words to his disciples before he

ascended to heaven, Jesus said, "You will receive power when the Holy Spirit comes on you; and you will be my witnesses in Jerusalem, and in all Judea and Samaria, and to the ends of the earth" (Acts 1:8). To the ends of the earth—that's everyone and everywhere! Yet, through his example, Jesus also shows us how to love one person at a time. Jesus could only physically be with one person or group of persons as he walked this earth in his human body. How did he love? He didn't spend all night making to-do lists of which people he would show love to the next day. He didn't have some kind of prioritization grid through which everyone who wanted his love had to pass. He simply loved people as the opportunity arose during the normal traffic patterns of his life. If he was in Jerusalem, he loved the people on the streets of Jerusalem. If he was traveling from Judea to Galilee, he loved the people he met along the way. When he was with his disciples, he showed love to them.

My wife, Chaundel, practices this command to love our neighbors better than anyone I know. She loves our neighbors literally—the people who live on our block. It's quite embarrassing to me how much better she is at this than I am! She finds out that one of our neighbors is in the hospital, and she's immediately there to visit them. She drops what she's doing to go next door and help a neighbor with a practical need. She commits to facing difficult and frightening circumstances with someone on our block. She goes for a walk in the neighborhood and meets a new neighbor also out walking—and the new neighbor is at a Bible study in our home the next week. I'm not making this up! I may speak to large numbers of people and be part of the pastoral team at a large church, but she is so much better than I am at doing what Jesus said is truly important. And she's involved in significant leadership and teaching ministries as well. I'd be jealous if I weren't married to her! Knowing that Chaundel can speak with great integrity about this command, I asked her, "What is it that causes you to consistently make the choice to love our neighbors?" She said, "I think it has something to do with making the most of the opportunity to build relationships and to let them know about someone who loves them a lot more than I do." Her response expresses a powerful motivation for love. Consistent love grows out of higher priorities and higher motivations. Consistent love can only be expressed one opportunity at a time.

> Consistent love can only be expressed one opportunity at a time.

Jesus had a purpose and a mission for his life — to bring salvation to all mankind. His life was directed by that purpose, and along each step of the journey he made the choice to love. To follow Jesus' example is to make the choice to love in the opportunities that arise in the everyday journey of life — as you raise your family, as you build your business, as you start your career, as you finish your education. At times in my life I've been so frustrated by the fact that I can't love everyone that I shrink back and don't act in love toward anyone. You don't want to take this depressing road. Make the choice to love the few you *can* love today, trusting in the greatness of God that he will put the right people in your path on the journey of life.

And be sure not to miss in Jesus' example his choice to spend time alone with God in order to be able to love others better. Jesus' choice to love included his choice to recharge and renew his heart and strength. Luke describes it this way: "Yet the news about [Jesus] spread all the more, so that crowds of people came to hear him and to be healed of their sicknesses. But Jesus often withdrew to lonely places and prayed" (Luke 5:15–16). Jesus spent time alone with the Father. If you are going to have healthy relationships, you'll need to spend time alone with God. Paradoxically, those who have the healthiest relationships often are the most comfortable in being alone with God.

It has always amazed me that Jesus would take so much time to be alone with the Father. He spent only thirty-three years on earth and only three years in public ministry, yet he spent significant portions of that time apart from people. Jesus had all of eternity to be alone with the Father. Why wouldn't he have spent every waking moment of his ministry with people? Because he knew it was important to his relationship with his Father and with others to make space to be alone. What you gain from time alone with God will strengthen every relationship in your life.

> "Dear friends, since God loved us that much, we surely ought to love each other."

The benefits to spending time alone with God don't come automatically. It's all too easy in those times to worry about what might go wrong or to lust for what you don't have. How do you spend time alone with God in a way that brings health to your life and relationships? For Jesus, time alone wasn't a way of escape; it wasn't a selfish right. It was a conversation. Even his time alone had a relational strength to it. He talked to the Father, and he listened to him. Jesus told the Father what was in his heart, and he listened for what was on the Father's heart. If you will follow this simple pattern, you will quiet your soul and broaden your perspective. You will focus your life. And you will strengthen your relationships through this decision to spend time alone with God.

Jesus Values Relationships!

Jesus places a high value on his relationship with us. How high a value? He died on the cross to make a relationship with him possible (see John 15:13). He wants us to be with him where he is for all eternity (see John 17:24). Look again at these two facts, and let them overwhelm you for just a moment: He died for you. He wants you to be with him.

The way in which Jesus values his relationship with us is one of the greatest motivations for pursuing stronger relationships with each other. John puts it this way: "Dear friends, since God loved us that much, we surely ought to love each other" (1 John 4:11 NLT).

As we conclude this week of looking at the priority of our love for God and our love for others, I invite you to join me in this prayer:

Lord, teach me to love you with all my heart, soul, mind, and strength. And teach me to love my neighbor as myself. I have a lot to learn. Right now, Lord, I bring to you a relationship that's on my mind. Would you lead me as I read this book and look at your example to see what to do and how to do it? This week, help me to see just one thing I can do that will make a difference. And Jesus, I can't close this prayer without thanking you for all you've done to create a relationship with me. You

know me and you love me and you gave your life for me.
Thank you for who you are. In your name. Amen.

DAY SEVEN
Thinking about My Relationships

Point to Ponder: Consistent love can only be expressed one opportunity at a time.

Verse to Remember: *Dear friends, since God loved us that much, we surely ought to love each other* (1 John 4:11 NLT).

Question to Consider: How can I show love to the person right in front of me—today?

Tomorrow: The impossible challenge

Love as Jesus Loves You

A new command I give you: Love one another. As I have loved you, so you must love one another.

John 13:34

8

The Impossible Challenge

overshadowed by more pressing feelings. As Jesus and his disciples enter the upper room, the air is filled with doubt and confusion. Jesus has told his followers that he was soon to die, but they did not understand. This confusion has created tension among them. To add to the tension, Jesus tells the disciples that one of them will betray him! It is a night of sideways glances, hushed conversations, and stubborn hearts.

In the midst of this all too human picture, Jesus begins to talk about something new. He shows his followers a new meaning to the traditional elements of the Passover meal—the bread and the wine. Of the bread, he says, "This represents my body that will be given for you"; of the wine, he says, "This represents my blood that will be shed for you." He speaks to them about a new promise between God and man that would be sealed by his blood.

Then Jesus gives his disciples a new commandment: "Love one another. As I have loved you, so you must love one another." In these few hours in the upper room, he repeats this simple command three times. He tenderly speaks, "Love one another." He simply states, "Love one another." He boldly commands, "Love one another."

Based on John 13:1-35

Jesus pointed us to the first commandment and second commandment. Now he gives us a new commandment. All three center on relationships. The first commandment centers on our relationship with God. The second centers on our

Principle #2: Love as Jesus Loves You

relationship with our neighbor. And the new commandment centers on our relationship with "one another."

Who is Jesus speaking of when he says "one another"? He was talking to his disciples when he gave this command — disciples who were very different from each other. The one thing they had in common was that they were followers of Jesus. When Jesus says "one another," he is talking about loving other people who have committed their lives to following Jesus Christ.

You may say, "OK, love other Christians — I think I can do that." But then come two little words that carry with them a seemingly insurmountable challenge: "As I." Jesus commands you to love others *as he loves you.* We're challenged to love as Jesus loved! When Jesus talked about love, he didn't say, "I want you to love the best you can." He said, "I want you to love as I have loved you." It's like someone inviting me to jump across the Grand Canyon. "Me, love as Jesus loved? You've got to be kidding. There's no way."

If I'm going to love as Jesus loved, I need the power that only Jesus can give.

Jesus didn't give us a "do the best you can" challenge; this is a "do more than you possibly could" challenge. If you're thinking, "The words are wonderful, but there's no way I'm going to be able to love as Jesus loved," that's a good thing. God has you right where he wants you. Recognizing the reality that you don't have the power to act with this kind of love is the first step. Jesus gave us this seemingly impossible challenge not to discourage us but to lead us to find the power to love others in him. If I'm going to love as Jesus loved, I need the power that only Jesus can give.

Our temptation is to want to change this "as I" principle into an "at least as good as" principle. Instead of "love as Jesus loved," we'd rather the standard be "love at least as good as those around you love." It feels a *lot* more comfortable to compare ourselves to others than it does to compare ourselves to Jesus! When comparing ourselves to other people, we think we can reach the goal of loving better in our own power. When Jesus becomes the standard, it is immediately obvious that we need a new relationship and power in our lives.

Jesus was fond of giving this kind of challenge — a challenge that invites his followers to see that God's power is the only answer. "Pour out your heart in prayer, and this mountain will be thrown into the sea" (see Mark 11:23). "Walk to me on the water" (see Matthew 14:28 – 29). These seem like impossible challenges.

Jesus gave one such challenge to all of us who have ever asked the question, "How many times do I have to forgive?"

EXPERIENCE THE TRUTH

Jesus was teaching in Capernaum, a small town by the Sea of Galilee. He talked to his followers about many things that day, including the importance of forgiving your brother. After Jesus had finished teaching, his disciple Peter took him aside to ask a question. Who knows, perhaps Jesus' words about forgiving a brother had sparked something in Peter's mind about a need to forgive his brother Andrew, who was also one of the disciples. Peter knew that many of the teachers of his day said that the maximum number of times one was required to forgive another person was three. With probably more than a little desire to impress, Peter said to Jesus, "Lord, how many times shall I forgive my brother when he sins against me? Up to seven times?" Behind his words could easily have been the thought, "Everyone else is saying three; how about seven, Jesus?" Something in Peter must have anticipated that Jesus was going to praise him for setting the bar of faith at such a stratospheric height.

Jesus' response must have floored Peter: "I tell you, not seven times, but seventy times seven."

It's as though Peter said, "Set the high jump bar at seven feet," and Jesus responded, "Try seven *miles*!" Why would Jesus do this? It seems that his answer would only discourage Peter. Peter was saying, "I'm willing to try my hardest," and Jesus responds, "Do the impossible!"

Based on Matthew 18:21 – 22

The answer to why Jesus would do this may surprise you. Jesus doesn't want you to try your hardest; Jesus wants you to learn to trust in him. Jesus set the bar so high that the only way it could be reached was by living and thinking in an entirely new way. Christianity is not trying harder; Christianity is trusting Jesus. Make no mistake: it's not a passive trust, sitting and waiting for God to act; it's a real trust, involving your whole heart, soul, mind, and strength.

We've all felt the sense of desperation that comes from running faster and getting nowhere, from trying harder and seeing no results. The greatest difficulties of life offer us our greatest opportunities to trust. I highly recommend this simple prayer: "Father, I don't have the strength to do this on my own. I'm trusting in your strength to enable me to believe and think and say and do the right thing. In Jesus' name. Amen."

Jesus is saying we need an external source of love. We need the power of Jesus Christ to love one another: *"As I have loved you, so you must love one another."*

Jesus told us this was a "new command." Don't skip over these words. There is a world of meaning here, igniting our power to love one another. It is a commandment. It is a commandment given by Jesus. It is a commandment that is new. We're going to spend the next couple of days unpacking these three sentences. In so doing, we'll begin to see how we can take up Jesus' "impossible" challenge to love.

Thinking about My Relationships

Point to Ponder: Jesus doesn't want us to try our hardest; he wants us to learn to trust in him.

Verse to Remember: *"A new command I give you: Love one another. As I have loved you, so you must love one another"* (John 13:34).

Question to Consider: How can I trust Jesus for the impossible in a relationship?

Tomorrow: The power of Jesus' command

The Power
of Jesus' Command

You cannot command an emotion, but you can command an action.

Understanding the difference between emotion and action — between what you feel and what you do — empowers every relationship you have. How do you love when you just don't feel you have it in you to love? Suppose you're thinking, "Of course I'd like to start feeling love again. Everything in me would like to start loving my husband [my wife] or even my kids again. Don't you think I've tried? I can't do it." Then Jesus comes along and says, "I *command* you to love in a new kind of way." How is this possible? How can Jesus command us to feel love? The fact is, he isn't! He is commanding us to *act* with love.

You can't command an emotion out of anyone. Picture this with a four-year-old. He's gotten a bright-red hand-knitted sweater as a birthday present from Grandma, and instead of being excited, he's crying. You say to him, "Be happy! I command you to be joyful about your gift." What happens?

The tears just flow more freely. We may learn to hide these kinds of responses as we get older, but we never outgrow them. You've had a tough day, and someone says, "I insist that you be happy." It doesn't work—it usually just makes you angry.

You can't command an emotion, but you can command an action. When Jesus says, "I command you to love one another," he's not saying, "*Feel* this way"; he's saying, "*Act* this way." Act with love toward another

Jesus commands us to act with love.

person. If you've fallen out of love or stopped loving altogether, the first step is to begin to act with love again. Remember which actions of love were once part of your relationship with your husband or wife or kids or friend? Act in that way again.

When faced with the challenge to act with love, no matter how we may feel, there is something in us that rebels. We think, "I don't feel right about that. I'd be such a phony to act with love toward someone when I don't feel love. It's not real if I don't feel like it. I'd be a hypocrite."

Yet we do things all the time that we don't feel like doing. If you woke up this morning and didn't feel like going to work, you wouldn't call and say, "I don't feel like being at work today, so I'm not coming. It would be very hypocritical for me to come to work this morning." No, you go in anyway—well, most of the time anyway! If we only did what we felt like doing, not much would ever get done.

Do you think Jesus *felt* like dying on the cross? Of course not. Jesus didn't face that morning thinking, "I feel like going to the cross today. I feel like experiencing the most excruciating pain, the most anguished disgrace, the most wrenching burden of mankind's sin." In fact, the night before his death, he prayed in Gethsemane, "Father, if you are willing, take this cup from me." In Jesus' prayer we see that he didn't follow his feelings. Instead, he prayed, "Yet not my will, but yours be done" (Luke 22:42).

I would call this kind of love *"nevertheless love."* Learn to pray as Jesus prayed — honestly telling God your feelings, and then saying, *"Nevertheless* not my will, but yours." This kind of love can only come from God. There are moments when not a single fiber of your being feels loving, and yet you act with love anyway. When your husband or wife has betrayed your trust and yet you love them anyway, that's nevertheless love. When your child has done the stupidest thing in human history — for the third week in a row — and yet you love them anyway, that's nevertheless love. When everything in you says, "Run away," or "Yell in anger," and yet you stay and talk, that's nevertheless love. That's acting with love. When Jesus was nailed to the cross and yet he looked at those who were crucifying him and said, "Father, forgive them," that was acting with love.

Are feelings part of the package of love? Of course — a sometimes wonderful, sometimes woeful part! But feelings don't get the deciding vote on how you will choose to act. Feelings tend to follow actions — sometimes quickly, sometimes slowly. When you begin to act with love again out of an obedient heart, feelings eventually follow.

What do you do when you feel like giving up? Those who make the greatest impact on this world aren't those who are the smartest, fastest, or richest; it's those who know what to do when they feel like giving up. We all face moments when we feel like giving up. I certainly have. I've often felt like giving up on my relationship with my dad.

My father has suffered with mental illness all of his life. As a direct result, our relationship has often been a struggle. When my mother died from cancer a number of years ago, Dad went into a real tailspin. He chose not to come to the funeral until about halfway through when he burst through the back doors of the church, yelled out a few words, and then left. *Chaotic* would have been the best word to describe our relationship at that point. He then disappeared. For years we didn't know where he was. For all I knew, he might have died. Then I heard from a family member that he'd been spotted—homeless and living on the streets of San Francisco. What a scary thing to hear about your dad! We tried to find him, but couldn't. Years later, he turned up again and eventually was placed at a good care facility. Dad and I began to write from time to time. It was strained at first but improved to the point where I was able to stop by and see him a few times. On one of my visits, I gave him two books: Rick Warren's book *The Purpose Driven Life* and a curriculum book on the core truths of the Christian faith that I'd cowritten called *Foundations*. Rick is my friend and boss, my pastor and brother-in-law. *The Purpose Driven Life* had sold about thirty-five million copies at that point, *Foundations* more like thirty-five copies. I'm happy to say that my dad liked my book better—he's still my dad!

Over the years, whenever my dad and I had the opportunity to talk about spiritual things, he expressed appreciation for what I was doing as a pastor but saw Christianity as a philosophy rather than as a personal relationship with God. I'd pretty much given up hope that he'd develop a

Principle #2: Love as Jesus Loves You

relationship with Jesus. After all, he was seventy-eight years old—if anything were going to happen, it would have already happened.

Then a letter came in the mail in which my dad wrote, "For years and years I refused to accept God, the Holy Spirit, and Jesus Christ. I worked on my sinful self my way without talking to God. Your words, Tom, in the *Foundations* book turned me about when you wrote, 'God is not some distant concept. Rather, God is near.' For six months I labored, seeking to preach to others, 'Do the right thing.' So now, Jesus is my guide. God says so." And on the back of the letter he wrote the words "Jesus saves lost souls."

Not giving up means you realize that Jesus takes whatever little we give him, and he does so much more!

I was seventeen years old when I became a believer in Jesus—and as I write this I'm fifty. So I've been praying for my dad and his relationship with God for thirty-three years. I'd like to say I never gave up hope—but I often needed others to encourage me. I'd like to say I prayed for him every day, but I prayed far too infrequently. I'd like to say I knew it would happen, but I ended up being gloriously surprised.

Jesus took the little I gave him—the prayers I did pray, the letters I did write, the hope I did have—and he did so much more. If you think not giving up means you have to be perfect and have it all together, it does not. Not giving up means you realize that Jesus takes whatever little we give him, and he does so much more!

Don't give up. Don't give up on people; the minute you do,

they'll surprise you. Don't give up on prayer; God is doing so much more through your prayers than you can see. Don't give up on God's promises. You have some dreams that are based on God's promises; don't give up on those dreams. When you feel like giving up, choose instead to act. Act on Jesus' command—and "love one another."

DAY NINE
Thinking about My Relationships

Point to Ponder: If you've stopped feeling love, the first step is to begin to act with love again.

Verse to Remember: *Let us not become weary in doing good, for at the proper time we will reap a harvest if we do not give up* (Galatians 6:9).

Question to Consider: Is there someone I don't feel like loving whom I need to love?

Tomorrow: The power of new

10

The Power
of New

Why did Jesus need to give his followers a *new* commandment? Weren't there already plenty of commandments in the Old Testament? Weren't the commands to love God and to love our neighbor enough?

This command of Jesus is "new" not so much in its content but in the way it is to be lived. There was an old way of doing things, and Jesus is telling his disciples that there must now be a new way of doing things. We all have our old ways of doing things, but Jesus wants to do something new in our lives. The old commandments were empowered in different ways from the new one. The old commandments were empowered by traditional habits—the way we've always done it; the new commandment is empowered by our dependence on God's power—the way Jesus did it. The old commandments were based on written rules; the new commandment is based on a living example—Jesus Christ. The old commandments were motivated by fear of the judgment God would bring on those who disobeyed; the new commandment is motivated by love: "There is no fear in love. But perfect love drives out fear, because fear has to do with punishment. The one who fears is not made perfect in love" (1 John 4:18).

This comparison of the old and the new applies to our relationships as well. Some relationships become old; some remain new. Some relationships degrade into habit, rules, "how we've always done it"; others continue to bask in the fresh air of newness, even after many years. If you had a ledger sheet with the word *old* on one side and the word *new* on the other, on which side would you place the most important relationships in your life? Where do you need to take a love that's old and make it new?

Jesus' new commandment is the key to renewing love. His command gives the path and the power for moving from old to new. Instead of just abiding by the letter of the law, you let the Spirit of the Lord begin to reign. Instead of just doing what you've always done, you begin to act with genuine concern for the other person. Instead of obeying a list of rules, you follow a living example.

How much of what you call love has become just a habit? You do what you do today because you did it yesterday — whether bathing your kids or going to work to support your family or giving an offering to the Lord. How can you renew a love that has grown old?

Rediscover the attitude of love in the everyday habits of your life.

Some think the only way to make something new is to start over. "Get a new wife, get a new family — that's the way to make things new," we think. It never works, of course, because this week's new becomes next week's old. Here instead is where to begin: rediscover the attitude of love in the everyday habits of your life. You simply take the things that have become mere habit and inject love into them again. Remember the expression of love that bubbled up as you enjoyed your first meal together as a couple? Remember the first time you picked up your new baby? Remember the love that was there at the beginning? Go back to that. Say to yourself as you do that routine task, "I'm doing this because I love him;" "I am acting with love as I do this for her." Try it for a week and see what happens. I cannot promise that this little step will solve every relational problem, but it will solve many of them; and it will get your heart to a place where you can find the strength to work on the other problems as well.

This is the way to renew even our relationship with God. When the believers who lived in Ephesus turned from their love for Jesus, Jesus' advice was, "Change your hearts and do what you did at first" (Revelation 2:5 NCV). The secret to renewing their love wasn't in some new thing they could discover or do; it was in doing the things they had done at the beginning with a new attitude that resulted from changed hearts.

Why is this so important? Because much of life is routine. If you don't allow love to become a part of the routine of life, love will be missing from the majority of the minutes in your day.

If you find yourself still wondering if you have the ability to make this daily choice to love, remember that this new commandment was given to us by Jesus. Jesus walked this earth as God in human flesh. No one knows us better than he does. And Jesus never commands us to do something he is not willing and able to empower us to do.

Whenever you see a command from God in the Bible,

it contains an implied promise. Why? Because God would never command you to do something he wouldn't give you the power to do. That would be cruel. Sometimes we think of God as sitting in heaven saying, "What can I do to really ruin their day today, to really make them feel guilty today?" That's *not* the way God thinks. Every time I see a command, I can say to myself, "I can do that by God's power."

Here are two stories to illustrate the effect of these two different ways of thinking — one about an engine trying to climb a mountain and another about a disciple trying to walk on water.

You remember the first story — *The Little Engine That Could.* This famous children's story told of the little engine that chanted "I think I can, I think I can" on its way to the top of a mountain. It's a wonderful children's story, but we shouldn't get our philosophy of the Christian life from it.

The second story comes from the Bible. It's the story of the disciple Peter, who took a walk on the water of the Sea of Galilee:

> Meanwhile, the disciples were in trouble far away from land, for a strong wind had risen, and they were fighting heavy waves.
>
> About three o'clock in the morning Jesus came to them, walking on the water. When the disciples saw him, they screamed in terror, thinking he was a ghost. But Jesus spoke to them at once. "It's all right," he said. "I am here! Don't be afraid."
>
> Then Peter called to him, "Lord, if it's really you, tell me to come to you by walking on water."
>
> "All right, come," Jesus said.

Principle #2: Love as Jesus Loves You

So Peter went over the side of the boat and walked on the water toward Jesus. But when he looked around at the high waves, he was terrified and began to sink. "Save me, Lord!" he shouted.

Instantly Jesus reached out his hand and grabbed him. "You don't have much faith," Jesus said. "Why did you doubt me?" And when they climbed back into the boat, the wind stopped.

Matthew 14:24-32 NLT

How did Peter walk on water for those few seconds? It certainly wasn't because Jesus told him to chant "I think I can, I think I can!" He walked on water by focusing on Jesus. It was when his focus moved from Jesus to the waves that he began to sink.

There are two different ways to live life—the "I think I can" life, and the "I know *I* can't, but I know *God* can" life. The first life is entirely dependent on your own motivation and energy. The attractive thing about this life is that because we are each wonderful creations of God, there are many things we *can* accomplish on our own. The problem with the "I think I can" life is that there's always another mountain to climb. And one day you're going to run into a mountain that you *can't* climb. "I think I can" will not get us over the most important mountains of life—facing our genuine inadequacies, our disconnection from God, and the reality of our own death. One of the most refreshing and energizing moments in any life is the moment someone says, "I know I can't, but I know God can. God can do in me what I cannot do for myself."

Thinking about My Relationships

Point to Ponder: God will never command you to do something he will not give you the power to do.

Verse to Remember: *There is no fear in love. But perfect love drives out fear, because fear has to do with punishment. The one who fears is not made perfect in love* (1 John 4:18).

Question to Consider: How can I take a love that's old and allow God to make it new?

Tomorrow: Feelings are important!

Feelings Are Important!

Of all the experiences we'll have as we watch the life and ministry of Jesus, perhaps the most perplexing comes in a single moment.

EXPERIENCE THE TRUTH

The news had just come to Jesus that Lazarus was near death. Along with his sisters, Mary and Martha, Lazarus was one of Jesus' closest friends. Jesus and his disciples stopped regularly at their home in the small town of Bethany on the outskirts of Jerusalem. After spending time facing the needy crowds and questioning leaders in Jerusalem, they found their trips to the home of these three to be welcome retreats.

And now Lazarus was very ill. In fact, Jesus told his disciples that he knew Lazarus had already died. When he had heard the news of Lazarus's illness, Jesus had done something totally unexpected. Instead of rushing to see Lazarus's sisters, Jesus waited two days before leaving for Bethany! This seems confusing. Why would Jesus wait to go to support this family he so obviously loved? When Jesus did arrive in Bethany, he saw the grief of his friends, and Jesus wept. Then his reason for waiting became clear. By the time Jesus finally got there, Lazarus had been in the tomb for four days. Jesus went to the tomb where Lazarus was buried. He asked that the stone covering the tomb be rolled aside. Then Jesus prayed a prayer of thanks to God and called for his friend Lazarus to come back to life: "Lazarus, come out!" And Lazarus walked out of the grave!

When Lazarus came out of that grave alive, it answered the question of why Jesus had waited. If he had arrived earlier, some would have said that Lazarus had recovered from an illness while in the tomb. But after four days in the tomb, there was no doubt that this was a genuine resurrection!

But then the truly perplexing thought hits: Why had Jesus wept? We know why Jesus waited. He waited because he knew he was going to bring Lazarus back to life. With that in mind, it might have made sense if Jesus had smiled knowingly when he saw others grieving Lazarus's death. Why the tears?

Based on John 11:1 - 44

As I consider this question, it becomes clear how much I have to learn about how emotions and faith and relationships connect. Jesus wept. He may have been overwhelmed by his

Principle #2: Love as Jesus Loves You

feeling for the pain that Lazarus had faced. Or he could have been thinking of the loss that had been so agonizing for Mary and Martha for a few days. Or he may simply have been expressing honestly his own emotions about death in that moment. Whatever the reason, Jesus did not act as though he was above it all. He wept. He took his own emotions seriously, and so he expressed those emotions openly and then chose to act lovingly.

This is a different picture of Jesus from the one many of us have. Jesus is often pictured as a transcendental Eastern mystic. Because of his deeper spiritual understanding, he is wrongly thought of as being emotionally distant from this world. Jesus, many think, lived on a higher plain, free from the encumbrance of emotions. Consider the way Jesus is often pictured in movies — wandering through the countryside in a kind of daze, as though he has no feelings whatsoever about what's going on around him.

This false picture causes us to equate spiritual strength with being emotionally distant. The message many of us hear is, "The more you deny your emotions, the more you will be like Jesus."

Yet when you look at Jesus' life, you see a man filled with emotion. You see his emotion in his tender compassion for a man ravaged by leprosy (Mark 1:40–42). You experience the depth of his feelings in his wrenching distress as he prays in Gethsemane about his impending death on the cross (Mark 14:33). You feel the emotion of gentle love Jesus has for his mother as he speaks to her from the cross (John 19:26–27). Jesus even openly expressed the emotion of anger — though to hear this makes some of us uncomfortable. Anger is an emotion, not a sin. What we do with our anger is often sinful, but it doesn't have to be. Jesus was angry when necessary, but he never sinned.

Jesus grew up in a Jewish culture that knew how to show emotion. When the Jews wept, it wasn't a little tear trickling down the cheek. They wept openly. They wailed loudly. They even tore their outer clothes into shreds to express their grief. Do you have an image of Jesus that rejects the idea he could so strongly express his emotions? Look at Hebrews 5:7 (NLT): "While Jesus was here on earth, he offered prayers and pleadings, with a loud cry and tears, to the one who could deliver him out of death. And God heard his prayers because of his reverence for God." With a loud cry and tears! This power of emotion prompted G. Walter Hansen to write these words in his classic article "The Emotions of Jesus":

> I am spellbound by the intensity of Jesus' emotions; not a twinge of pity, but heartbroken compassion; not a passing irritation, but terrifying anger; not a silent tear, but groans of anguish; not a weak smile, but ecstatic celebration. Jesus' emotions are like a mountain river, cascading with clear water. My emotions are more like a muddy foam or feeble trickle. Jesus invites us to come to him and drink. Whoever is thirsty and believes in him will have the river of his life flowing out from the innermost being (John 7:37–38). We are not to be merely spellbound by what we see in the emotional Jesus; we are to be unbound by his Spirit so that his life becomes our life, his emotions our emotions, to be "transformed into his likeness with ever-increasing glory."*

---

*G. Walter Hansen, "The Emotions of Jesus," *Christianity Today* 41, no. 2 (February 3, 1997): 43.

The example as we look at the life of Jesus is clear: Jesus did not deny his emotions; he denied himself by not always bowing to those emotions. He took his emotions *very* seriously, and he teaches us to do the same. He teaches us to act in ways that recognize the importance of our feelings. If you don't see the importance of expressing and dealing with your feelings, those feelings can end up controlling your life. Denial of your feelings gives them a power over you that God never intended them to have. It's only as you see the importance of your feelings that you can begin to act in ways that keep those feelings from running your life.

Feelings by themselves can sometimes lead you down a good road. But more often than not, they'll lead you right into a train wreck. How many people have you talked to who "felt" that a (now disastrous) dating relationship was going to be perfect, or who "felt" that starting their own (now bankrupt) business would be the fulfillment of all their dreams.

We live in a world where many act solely in response to their feelings. It doesn't matter who they hurt along the way or what commitments they break; if their feelings tell them to do something, then that's what they'll do. In reaction to this rampant immaturity, it's easy to think the right thing to do would be to ignore your feelings and act on purely logical conclusions about what is right—which you could do, except for one small problem: you're human! Humans have feelings, and these feelings are going to influence your life. Jesus, who was fully human and fully God, neither ignored nor was

> *Jesus did not deny his emotions; he denied himself by not always bowing to those emotions.*

controlled by his feelings. He expressed his feelings in ways that opened the door for others to have faith.

As a picture of the difference between being governed by your feelings and being strengthened to act by your feelings, consider the lives of two Ernests — well-known author Ernest Hemingway and little-known missionary Ernest Fowler. Ernest Hemingway is universally acclaimed as one of the great American authors. Brimming with natural talent, his life was governed almost entirely by what he felt like doing at any given moment. In the end, he shot himself to death (as did his father before him and his brother after him), because that's what his depression drove him to feel like doing. It's amazing that with such a tragic end, there are still some today who look to emulate his lifestyle. His was a life and talent wasted, because in the end he could not control the emotions that had governed him.

Five years after Hemingway's death, missionary Ernest Fowler also died of a gunshot wound. His was not self-inflicted but came at the hands of bandits who attacked his missionary home and family. Fowler and his family had moved to northeastern Colombia in order to reach out to the Motilon Indians — a tribe that had been close to his heart since he had first hacked his way through the jungle to meet them in 1943.

On a fateful day in July of 1966, Earnest had taken his daughter Valerie and their live-in household helper on a picnic. The Fowlers' son Johnny had his fourteen-year-old friend David Howard over to visit. Now a seminary professor, David gave an eyewitness account of the events of that day in a sermon he preached in 1994. He tells of seven men who came to the Fowlers' home dressed as policemen — but they were bandits, not policemen. It was the practice of the bandits in this region to rob a house, kill everyone inside, and then burn it to the ground. But on this day, they robbed the home, locked everyone in a small washroom, and left.

As they fled down the path away from the home, the bandits met Earnest and the two girls returning from their picnic. In the end, one of the bandits fired two shots at Ernest, and he died instantly. The girls escaped unharmed and made their way back to the Fowler home, where they informed everyone what had happened. The family rushed to the place where Ernest lay dead, and they carried the body back to their home.

After the funeral, David Howard recalls hearing Fowler's wife capture the spirit of her husband's life with the words, "Ernest was always ready to step aside for those in a hurry to get ahead, and step back to help and encourage those who were lagging behind."

Howard summed up his own lessons from this experience this way: "Ernest Fowler did make a difference, because he was faithful in all things, large and small. Ernest Fowler got dirty many times and served others his whole life.... Ernest Fowler was 'faithful, even to the point of death' in his ministry for Christ and his concern for others."[*]

Ernest Hemingway took his life; Ernest Fowler gave his life. The author's emotions drove him to a life of excitement and excess; the missionary's heart called him to go to a dangerous place and serve a people noticed by very few others, a people whom God dearly loved. One man's emotions drove him to destruction; the other's called him to sacrifice.

---

[*]David M. Howard Jr., "Ernest Fowler: Faithful unto Death and Making a Difference," from a sermon preached at Camp-of-the-Woods, Speculator, New York, August 26, 1994, *http://www.bethel.edu/%7Edhoward/personal/ efFaithfulUntoDeath.htm.*

Thinking about My Relationships

Point to Ponder: Jesus took his own emotions seriously, and so he expressed those emotions openly and then chose to act lovingly.

Verse to Remember: *Jesus wept* (John 11:35).

Question to Consider: Is there a feeling in my life that I haven't dealt with?

Tomorrow: Act immediately, act radically

12

Act Immediately,
Act Radically

To love as Jesus loved, I must act as Jesus acted. Jesus didn't treat his emotions as an invitation to focus on himself but as a call to love others. As I looked at the example and teaching of Jesus while reading through the Gospels, I discovered two principles for dealing with the emotional side of our lives: first, give your heart priority by acting immediately, and second, take your heart seriously by acting radically.

Give Your Heart Priority
by Acting Immediately

Most of us feel like our actions are important, but too few of us act like our feelings are important. Instead of dealing with our feelings, we too easily excuse them, nurse them, or try to ignore them. It's interesting that no matter which of these strategies we try, the end result is the same: the feelings invariably grow stronger because we have not dealt with them.

So how do you give your heart priority? How do you act like your feelings are important?

In his Sermon on the Mount, Jesus provides us with practical insight. He talks about what to do if you are giving an offering at church and suddenly remember that someone has something against you. Jesus says, "First go and be reconciled to your brother; then come and offer your gift" (Matthew 5:24).

Focus on that word *first*. You may even want to circle it. Jesus is talking about priorities. "First go ...." If there's a relationship going wrong, give it priority. There's nothing more important. Recognize what's in your heart, and do something about it. You give your heart priority when you act immediately. In fact, you may need to put this book down right now and *act immediately* to strengthen a relationship.

What do you need to do before you read even one more sentence? Do it *now*.

You may be thinking, "What if I've failed to act at the time the relationship went wrong? It was something that happened a long time ago. Has the opportunity been lost?" No, you can still act immediately *now*!

> If you don't act immediately, your emotions will fester inside until they become destructive.

Why is it so important to act immediately? Because if you don't, your emotions will fester inside until they become destructive. Emotions are meant to be *instructive*, not *destructive*. They should tip us off to actions we need to take. But when we bottle them up inside, they grow to a point where they begin to motivate actions that can tear our relationships apart. In Jesus' Sermon on the Mount, he uses a good portion

Principle #2: Love as Jesus Loves You

of his message to talk about the importance of both how you act on the outside and what you feel on the inside. For instance, Jesus says, "You have heard that it was said to the people long ago, 'Do not murder'" (Matthew 5:21). That's the outside action— *"Don't do that."* But then Jesus takes it a step further. "I tell you that anyone who is angry with his brother will be subject to judgment" (5:22).

The word for "angry" here suggests a settled anger, a malice nursed inwardly—an anger that has been fed in order to help it to grow. We all know the difference between dealing with our anger and feeding our anger. It's easy to lie to ourselves and pretend we're keeping our anger inside. We tell ourselves, "So what if I hate the people in my office. Big deal if I feel trapped in my marriage. So what if I look at my kids and nurse feelings of disappointment toward them. What they don't know won't hurt them." Not true! Your heart always leaks out into your actions.

Think you can hide what's in your heart? It's impossible— it will eventually leak out. It's like having a radioactive container with just a small hole in it. The leak is inevitable, and always destructive—which is why it is so important that we act immediately.

Have you noticed how quickly husbands and wives pick up on this "leaking out" of the true feelings of the heart? Your face may look just a little too innocent; your husband or wife may notice a particular twitching of your nose and say, "What's wrong?" You say, "Nothing's wrong," when you know in your heart that something's wrong—and he or she knows it too.

The heart always leaks out. It's like the irritating high-pitched sound of air leaking out of a balloon. Some of us are quite good at holding negative feelings in for a while. The balloon keeps getting bigger and bigger; but along comes the slightest irritation and — blam! — your heart *explodes* out.

Your emotions don't have to inevitably lead to an explosion. Give the feelings of your heart priority, and act immediately.

Take Your Heart Seriously by Acting Radically

One of the most radical statements Jesus ever made was this: "If your right hand causes you to sin, cut it off and throw it away" (Matthew 5:30). Obviously Jesus is talking about our heart attitudes and not merely our hands. If you were to cut off your right hand and still wanted to sin, you could sin with your left hand just as well. Jesus is telling us not to let *anything* get in the way of the radical heart change he wants to work in our lives. Throughout the Bible, the "right hand" is a picture of that which is most important, most precious, most valued.

What you allow into your heart is serious business. So take it seriously. Be willing to say, "I will do anything it takes to ensure that my heart is in the right place."

What you allow into your heart affects every relationship. So when you recognize some unforgiveness, some bitterness, some lust in your heart, don't try to just taper it off. Cut it off as quickly as possible because what's happening in your heart is having a negative impact on your relationships with God and others. Jesus reminds us of how crucial this is when he says, "Cut off your right hand." Take your heart seriously by acting radically.

As a pastor I have counseled couples who are dealing with the temptation to marital unfaithfulness. Using a composite of these couples to give a glimpse at how such a conversation may go, suppose that Carol and George have agreed to meet with their pastor:

CAROL: I know our marriage hasn't been all that it should be. And for some time now I've felt that George has been growing emotionally distant from me. And then I found this birthday card that a female coworker wrote to George, and the language she used seemed like they were much more than just coworkers.

GEORGE: Carol confronted me with the card, and I admitted that this women and I had been going out to lunch for the last few months. I've talked with her in ways I know I shouldn't have. We haven't crossed the line physically, but I've said things to her that I know are too intimate. I know I'm getting emotionally close to her and that I'm playing with fire.

PASTOR: George, you're right. The emotions you're dealing with are powerful, and you must take them seriously. For your marriage to survive, I encourage you to make the decision today to break off all contact with this woman.

GEORGE: I know logically that what you're saying is right, Pastor. You asked us to be brutally honest as this meeting began, and so I have to say that I just don't know if I can do that. These feelings I have for her are just so *real*.

PASTOR: George, you are the one who has created that

reality. You chose to meet alone with a woman who wasn't your wife, to build emotional bonds with her, and to share a secret sin with her. The question is, are you going to let the emotions you've built determine your future, or are you going to choose to do what is right and to ask God to build a new set of emotions into your heart? Will you choose your relationship with this woman, or will you choose your marriage?

Having walked through this with a number of people, I can tell you that when answering the question of what they will choose, the majority want to choose both. They'll suggest something like, "Maybe I could only see this woman at work in our meetings, and my wife and I will go to counseling to work on our marriage." Because the pain of dealing with their feelings is so great, they want to take the easy way out and pretend that these feelings aren't really an issue.

You may think that allowing your mind to wander even briefly to a temptation toward adultery will not affect your marriage. Jesus says it will. You may think that the feelings of anger you're nursing are not affecting your relationships. Jesus says, "Yes, they are." What's happening in your heart is serious business. You may think that the self-pity you heap on yourself every day isn't affecting your relationships. But it is.

When we hear Jesus say, "Cut it off," we sometimes feel we don't know how. "I can't change my heart," we say to ourselves. "I'd love to do that, but I can't change the way I feel." You're right; you cannot change the way you feel. But you can change the circumstances that are causing the way you feel. And then the feelings will change.

When someone talks to any of our pastors about being tempted toward an adulterous affair, we always advise him or her to change the circumstances to escape the temptation. Sexual temptation is a very powerful temptation, and God's advice is that we don't try to battle this temptation in hand-to-hand combat. He tells us to get as far away from it as we can: "Run away from sexual sin! No other sin so clearly affects the body as this one does. For sexual immorality is a sin against your own body" (1 Corinthians 6:18 NLT). So leave your job and go to a different job, if that's what it takes. Leave the neighborhood you're living in and go to a different neighborhood, if that's what it takes. Is staying at your job worth losing your marriage? Is the neighborhood you're living in worth losing a relationship God has meant to last for a lifetime?

What's happening in your heart is serious business.

You may think, "I can handle it; I can handle these feelings." But Jesus is saying, "Cut it off!" What you've allowed into your heart is serious business, and it's going to affect your life. Take your heart seriously, and be willing to act radically.

Thinking about My Relationships

Point to Ponder: Your emotions are meant to be instructive, not destructive.

Verse to Remember: *"If your right hand causes you to sin, cut it off and throw it away. It is better for you to lose one part of your body than for your whole body to go into hell"* (Matthew 5:30).

Question to Consider: How do I need to act immediately or act radically in order to make the choice to love?

Tomorrow: Choose to fellowship, choose to forgive

13

Choose to Fellowship, Choose to Forgive

Relationships are like competing in the Indy 500. We're not talking about a lazy trip down some quiet country road. Relationships are complicated, high-speed stuff. The smallest misjudgment can cause us to spin out. To be successful in the Indy 500, you need a professional driver. When it comes to relationships, there's only one professional who drove this course—Jesus. He's the one who made relationships, and he's the one who can empower them and steer them in the right direction. Jesus said, "Love each other as I have loved you" (John 15:12). He wants to give you his power to love in a new and better way.

Much of what we call love is actually polite selfishness. We say, "I love you," but we really mean, "I love you because …" "Because of what you do for me, because you're pretty, because you're handsome, because you're smart, because you're rich." Or we really mean, "I love you if …" "If you meet my needs, if you're not too much trouble." Or we mean, "I love you when …"

"When I'm successful, when I've had a good day, when I feel like it."

Jesus calls us to a higher kind of love. We were never meant to do it on our own. "As I have loved you," Jesus said. Jesus Christ can give a power in your relationships that you never dreamed possible—power to love and grow, power so that you are not relationally worn down at the end of every day.

What exactly will Jesus give you the power to do? As you flip through the pages of the New Testament, you'll find yourself regularly coming across challenges to love like Jesus in specific ways. Jesus is your example. The way he loves you models the way you are to love others. The Bible is filled with ways you can begin to practice this "as I" kind of love. Today and tomorrow we're going to look at four of the most powerful of these choices we are all challenged to make.

Choose to Fellowship

To love as Jesus loved, we are to choose to fellowship. The apostle John declared, "If we are living in the light of God's presence, just as Christ is, then we have fellowship with each other" (1 John 1:7 NLT).

Look up the word *fellowship* on Dictionary.com, and you'll find that it means "the companionship of individuals in a congenial atmosphere." "Companionship" fellowship means you must actually spend time with other people; "congenial" fellowship means you *enjoy* spending time with these people. It's easy to say you love if you're spending most of your time alone. You can only truly love when spending time with others.

Let's admit it, there are many high-tech barriers to fellowship today. Even though you're with people, you're not really with them. You're talking on the phone but reading your email at the same time. You're on a walk with a friend, and both of you have your iPod headphones on. You're out on a date—in a movie theater where you can't talk. We're at a point where we need to disconnect in order to connect—to disconnect from our media sources in order to connect with people.

> Much of what we call love is actually polite selfishness.

The greatest barriers to fellowship, however, aren't in our technology; they are in our thinking. We misunderstand and minimize the meaning of fellowship. It's no wonder we do this. *Fellowship* is a word used mostly in churches, where it refers to a dingy room (the "Fellowship Hall") in the back of the church where people go to drink coffee out of small Styrofoam cups. Not only is the coffee better at the local Starbucks; usually the fellowship is too.

True fellowship cannot be forced or scheduled; it must be chosen and accepted. Find someone who is making the attempt to follow Jesus in his or her life, someone you would actually enjoy being with. Take the risk to talk to them about a doubt you're facing, a struggle you're having, a joy you're experiencing. *Now* you're fellowshipping!

Choose to Forgive

To love as Jesus loved, not only are we to choose to fellowship; we are also to choose to forgive. The apostle Paul urged, "Be kind and compassionate to one another, forgiving each other, just as in Christ God forgave you" (Ephesians 4:32). I often hear people say, "I just can't forgive." I've learned to ask two questions when I hear this statement. The first is, "What do you think it means to forgive?" People often feel they can't forgive because they don't understand forgiveness. Someone has told them that forgiveness means forgetting—and they know they just cannot forget. But the truth is, forgiveness doesn't mean you have to pretend you don't remember the fact that something happened. No one could forgive if that was what forgiveness meant. Forgiveness means you let it go. You let go of your bitterness and your desire for revenge.

Neither does forgiveness mean trusting a person to the extent that he or she can hurt you again. There is a vast difference between forgiveness and trust. If I'm going to follow the example of Jesus, I must forgive immediately—whether the other person asks it of me or not. But trust is rebuilt over time. If someone steals money from you, you forgive them as soon as you find out; but a lot of trust will need to be rebuilt before he or she would be left alone with your money again.

The second question is, "Who are you trying to punish by choosing not to forgive?" If you're not careful, you'll find yourself thinking you have to hang on to the hurt so you can punish someone for what they've done to you or to someone you love. Of course you're really only punishing yourself. The one who has hurt you likely doesn't even know—or care—what you think. It's tearing you up inside, while the person who hurt you goes obliviously on his or her way. Through your bitterness, that past pain hurts you over and over again. This bitterness hurts all of your other relationships, including your relationship with God. Jesus said, "When you are praying, first forgive anyone you are holding a grudge against, so that your Father in heaven will forgive your sins, too" (Mark 11:25 NLT). If you think you can choose not to forgive someone else and not have it affect your relationship with God, you're lying to yourself.

If you are struggling to forgive, you are not alone. Jesus understands, and he gives you a prescription. He told a story about a servant who was forgiven a debt of millions of dollars but couldn't forgive someone who owed him just a few hundred dollars. At the end of the story, Jesus related what happened to the servant who could not forgive:

> "Then the king called in the man he had forgiven and said, 'You evil servant! I forgave you that tremendous debt because you pleaded with me. Shouldn't you have mercy on your fellow servant, just as I had mercy on you?' Then the angry king sent the man to prison until he had paid every penny.
> "That's what my heavenly Father will do to you if you refuse to forgive your brothers and sisters in your heart."
>
> Matthew 18:32–35 NLT

No fluffy, marshmallow language from Jesus on this one. He goes straight to the heart of the problem and frankly declares that our refusal to forgive someone can always be traced back to a misunderstanding of our own need for forgiveness and grace from God. There is a breath of fresh air in this hard-to-hear truth. If you're struggling to forgive, resist the temptation to focus on your feelings of guilt about that struggle; focus instead on God's grace and magnify in your mind his great forgiveness of your sins. I've found that the only way I can find the strength to forgive others is to embrace the fact that Jesus has forgiven me.

If you're not sure that God has forgiven you, this is the place to start. Twice in my life I've had the opportunity to serve on a jury. After our deliberations I couldn't help but lock my eyes on the defendant as the verdict was read. Talk about a hot seat! We all sit in private courtrooms every day, having to listen to a voice inside rendering a verdict on the actions of our lives. We all live with a verdict of guilty. Something in our past. Something in our thoughts. Some secret no one else knows. The gavel comes down, and the voice inside us declares, "Guilty." How do you handle this verdict?

One of first promises I was taught as a new Christian was this verse from Scripture: "God is faithful and reliable. If we confess our sins, he forgives them and cleanses us from everything we've done wrong" (1 John 1:9 GWT). I was taught to trust God instead of myself for forgiveness. God has plenty of good things he wants us to do, but these good deeds are a *response* to his grace and not a way to earn his grace. It's a pipe dream to think we could do enough good things to earn God's favor. The apostle Paul wrote, "You did not save yourselves; it was a gift from God. It was not the result of your own efforts, so you cannot brag about it. God has made us what we are. In Christ Jesus, God made us to do good works, which God planned in advance for us to live our lives doing" (Ephesians 2:8–10 NCV). Forgiveness is God's gift to us. Start by receiving this gift. You receive this gift by offering to God a

> The only way you can find the strength to forgive others is to embrace the fact that Jesus has forgiven you.

Principle #2: Love as Jesus Loves You

prayer of trust. "Father, I trust in you for forgiveness instead of trusting myself to earn your favor. I trust you to show me how to live the life you created me to live." Accept God's gift. Then respond by passing the gift on to others.

Thinking about My Relationships

Point to Ponder: The only way I can find the strength to forgive others is to embrace the fact that Jesus has forgiven me.

Verse to Remember: *God is faithful and reliable. If we confess our sins, he forgives them and cleanses us from everything we've done wrong* (1 John 1:9 GWT).

Questions to Consider: How can I take my experiences of fellowship a step deeper? Who is the person in my life I need to forgive?

Tomorrow: Choose to accept, choose to sacrifice

14

Choose to Accept, Choose to Sacrifice

The Bible is clear about exactly what it means to love as Jesus loved. God didn't want to leave us stumbling around in the dark. Yesterday we reflected on the reality that loving as Jesus loved means you make the choice to fellowship and the choice to forgive. Today we focus on two other challenges seen in the example of Jesus: love makes the choice to accept, and love makes the choice to sacrifice.

Choose to Accept

To love as Jesus loved, we are to choose to accept. The apostle Paul counsels, "Accept one another, then, just as Christ accepted you, in order to bring praise to God" (Romans 15:7). We accept one another as Jesus accepts us. Why is this important? Because all relationships are based on acceptance—even though we tend to think they're based on similarities. "If only you were just more like I am," we think, "our relationship would be better." Unity isn't found in being the same. The strongest relationships often occur with those who are most different—those who have learned to accept their differences instead of demanding that others become just like them. Unless you accept others' differences, you are doomed to spend the rest of your life only with people who are just like you. Now that's a scary thought! Without people around you who are different from you, you'll never truly grow.

One of the most important lessons I've had to learn is the difference between acceptance and forgiveness. There are many differences with others that have nothing to do with forgiveness; they are simply issues of acceptance. When someone has a viewpoint on an issue that is different from the one I have, I need to accept him, not forgive him. When someone's personality causes her to deal with a situation in a different way from how I would handle it, I need to accept her, not forgive her. I've seen that this issue of acceptance may be most important when we face a grief together. We all grieve in very different and very personal ways. One person is quiet and reflective, while another needs to talk nonstop. One moves past the grief quite quickly, while another has the grief hit months later. When you're grieving a loss, it's tempting to feel that everyone around you must grieve as you do. To love as Jesus loved is to make the choice to accept our differences.

Without people around you who are different from you, you'll never truly grow.

Choose to Sacrifice

To love as Jesus loved, we must choose to sacrifice. It's a fourth mark of loving—fellowship, forgiveness, acceptance, and now sacrifice. The apostle John declares, "This is how we know what love is: Christ gave his life for us. We too, then, ought to give our lives for others!" (1 John 3:16 TEV).

True love sacrifices. The greatest sacrifices may not be the once-in-a-lifetime sacrifices; they may well be the daily sacrifices. You give up your way and seek another person's good. No one else may even know you did it, but you'll know you acted in response to Jesus' love for you.

What do these daily sacrifices look like? Up until now, many of our examples from Jesus have been about what to do in a relational conflict or temptation. Do you have to wait until you get into trouble to begin to strengthen your relationships? Of course not! There are positive steps you can take each day to revolutionize the way you love those around you.

Picture it this way: instead of waiting until you must choose surgery, you can do daily exercises to keep your relational heart healthy. Based on the description of love in 1 Corinthians 13, I've outlined below five practical exercises you can do for your heart each day. Most of what you'll see here won't be new; after all, new information isn't really the point. What we're seeking is changes in the way we act in our families, churches, workplaces, and schools.

The greatest sacrifices may well be the daily sacrifices.

1. Be Patient: "Love Is Patient" (1 Corinthians 13:4)

Patience involves the often difficult art of waiting. We have thousands of opportunities to practice patience. Here are a few examples to jog your thinking:

- When you are ready before your spouse and children are ready, you don't get in the car and circle the cul-de-sac — honking the horn every time around! Love is patient.
- When your kids are engaged in a project and struggling, you don't jump in and say, "Let me do it for you!" even though with every fiber of your being you want to get it done faster. You help *them* to do it. Love is patient.
- When other people are talking, you don't finish their sentences for them. I confess that I often fail at this opportunity to express patience. You know what they're going to say, so you just say it for them — you're moving the conversation along. But maybe, just maybe, they wanted to be able to say it themselves — or maybe the thought was quite different from the one you thought they were thinking. Love is patient.

We can find no better example of genuine patience than in God's love toward us. Think of this: God listens to *all* of our prayers. As halting as they may be, even though he knows in advance what we are going to say, God listens to every word. This is his promise from Scripture: "We can be confident that he will listen to us whenever we ask him for anything in line with his will" (1 John 5:14 NLT).

2. Be Kind: "Love Is Kind" (1 Corinthians 13:4)

Kind is one of the most powerful words in a relationship. It may sound so small, but it's a word that can help heal the deepest hurt and strengthen the weakest relationship. Kindness is expressed in the doing of the little things—and the little things add up to a great relationship. Kindness means we recognize and meet someone's need in a practical way. Kindness means taking the grand vows we make to one another in a marriage ceremony and expressing them in the practical ways of washing dishes, taking out garbage, and vacuuming living rooms—even when it's not your turn. Kindness means turning the great hopes and dreams as we gaze on our adorable newborn in a hospital nursery into changing diapers and staying up all night with a sick child. Kindness is turning our great plans to "change the world" into serving hungry people in a soup kitchen or visiting the sick in a quiet hospital room.

As English poet William Wordsworth has written, this may be "that best portion of a good man's life, his little, nameless, unremembered acts of kindness and of love."*

3. Don't Be Proud: "[Love] Does Not Envy, It Does Not Boast, It Is Not Proud" (1 Corinthians 13:4)

Alongside the words *envy*, *boast*, and *proud*, place the word *insecurity*. If you felt truly secure in God's love for you, you would have nothing to envy, you wouldn't need to boast, and you wouldn't have to build your ego by feeding it heaping helpings of pride.

---

*William Wordsworth, *Tintern Abbey*.

Security is a Mount Everest–sized issue in relationships. Take even the best relationship and add a little bit of insecurity, and you'll create stress. In this light, ask yourself, "What am I doing to add even a degree of insecurity to a relationship?" Maybe you're hiding something—some feeling, some fact—from your spouse. Maybe you're not consistent in disciplining your kids so they haven't a clue what's coming next. Maybe you haven't spoken to someone in a really long time. The real issue behind each of these choices is our pride. What one step can you take today to make a relationship more secure? Think of the difference it can make for you to call someone today and say, "No matter what happens, I will always love you."

4. Don't Be Selfish: "[Love] Is Not Rude, It Is Not Self-Seeking, It Is Not Easily Angered, It Keeps No Record of Wrongs" (1 Corinthians 13:5)

Is it hard for you to tell when you're being selfish? It is for me. When I'm being selfish, I'm focused on myself, not on whether or not I'm being selfish. I don't know of a better list of the signs of selfishness than these four characteristics listed in 1 Corinthians 13:5. Being rude, seeking your own interests, expressing anger quickly, keeping a record of wrongs—all of these signal a selfish heart.

These warning signs tell us, "I'm centering on myself; I've got to get back to centering on Christ so I can center on others." You're selfish; so am I. What are we going to do about it? Selfishness is such an all-pervasive problem that it's easy to sink into discouraged defeat. But overexamining our own selfishness can also be selfish, because the focus is still on us! The only way to deal with selfishness is by choosing to be unselfish, one day at a time, one action at a time.

5. Don't Give Up: "[Love] Always Protects, Always Trusts, Always Hopes, Always Perseveres"
(1 Corinthians 13:7)

The word *persevere* has a compelling picture behind it in the Greek language—the picture of soldiers who, when the enemy was approaching, would tie their leg to a fellow soldier. By so doing, if fear were to overtake them, they wouldn't find themselves running away and leaving their friend to fight the battle alone. They literally bound themselves together so they could fight the battle together.

You may be right on the edge of quitting in a relationship. Hear again from Scripture encouraging truth about the power of love: "It always protects, always trusts, always hopes, always perseveres." Who do you need to decide to bind yourself to? Say these words to them: "I'll face this with you. I believe in you. I'll look forward to the future with you. Even when every bone in my body wants to run and hide, we're bound together. I will stay with you, and we'll overcome together."

Do you wonder if you can really make the personal changes that will allow you to love as Jesus loved? The one who recorded for us Jesus' command to "love one another" certainly changed! Jesus gave the apostle John, along with his brother James, the nickname "Sons of Thunder" (Mark 3:17) when they were young men. They were loud, opinionated, pushy, and prideful. In his later years, John became known as "the disciple whom Jesus loved" (John 13:23). In his short letter of 1 John, he uses the word *love* more than any other New Testament letter does. What brought about the change? I believe it was what happened in the upper room on the night before Jesus died on the cross. When John heard Jesus speak the words "Love one another," his heart and life were changed. Those words became the theme of the rest of his life, as evidenced by how often he repeats them in his writings.

John got it! When other believers around him began to divide over details, John loved like Jesus and encouraged fellowship and acceptance. When his brother James was the first believer to be martyred for his faith, John loved like Jesus and forgave. When he as an old man faced exile for his faith, John loved like Jesus and sacrificed. These words of Jesus, empowered by the person of Jesus, changed the entire direction of John's life. They can change your life too.

As this week's look at loving as Jesus loved concludes, I invite you to join me in this prayer:

Lord, I need to grow in my relationships. I pray that I never get beyond being challenged by this incredible promise that I can love others as you loved us. As I hear the challenge in these words, I choose to turn to you and ask you for the strength to love. As I pray this, I recognize how deeply you love me. I pray that the love you have for me will motivate a love for others that I could never have on my own. In your name I pray, Jesus. Amen.

Thinking about My Relationships

Point to Ponder: The greatest sacrifices love makes may not be the once-in-a-lifetime sacrifices but may well be the daily sacrifices.

Verse to Remember: *[Love] always protects, always trusts, always hopes, always perseveres* (1 Corinthians 13:7).

Questions to Consider: Whom do I need to accept in love? How and to whom can I express love through patience, kindness, humility, unselfishness, and perseverance?

Tomorrow: Communication isn't easy!

Communicate
from the Heart

Out of the overflow of the heart the mouth speaks.
Matthew 12:34

15

Communication
Isn't Easy!

Merriam-Webster's online dictionary defines *communication* as "a process by which information is exchanged between individuals through a common system of symbols, signs, or behavior."* With apologies to Mr. Webster, haven't you found the real-life definition to read more like this: "a process by which information is confused by individuals through a conflicting system of emotions, behaviors, backgrounds, and desires"?

Who hasn't fallen into the communication twilight zone? You're having a talk with your spouse, a coworker, one of your children, or a close friend. Communication seems to be at an all-time high until "the wrong word" slips out of someone's mouth. All of a sudden, the conversation starts to heat up like a nuclear reactor headed for a meltdown. Seemingly powerless to stop it, we find ourselves arguing or — even worse — not talking at all.

---

*Merriam-Webster Online Dictionary, *http://www.m-w.com/dictionary/ communication* (January 2, 2008).

As a young pastor, I once tried to encourage one of the church's administrative assistants, who was having a bad day. I *meant* to say to her, "You are much more indispensable around here than you think." But the words came out, "You're not as indispensable as you tend to think you are." It took us a while to sort that one out!

Why is communication so important to relationships? Because *all relationships are fueled by communication.* Just as a car will never reach its destination without fuel, our relationships are guaranteed to go nowhere without communication. Lack of communication has kept some relationships stuck in the garage for decades; others find that they get off to a great start but then run out of gas a short way down the road. It takes good communication to keep a relationship moving ahead for a lifetime.

Just as your car needs the right kind of fuel to make it down the road, your relationships need the right kind of communication to make it through life. What would happen to your car if you put water—or battery acid—into the gas tank? It's even more vital to make sure we put the right kind of communication into our relationships.

I hate it when people try to make communication sound simple. It isn't! I have a book on my shelf with the subtitle *How to Say Anything in 30 Seconds.* It's a 120-page book—obviously it took the author a lot more than 30 seconds to say how to say anything in 30 seconds!

My daughter, Alyssa, once called me when I was in the middle of writing a sermon about communication.

"Do we have any wing nuts?" she asked. "We have to build a motor for Physics."

"No," I said, "you'll have to go buy some. And make sure you get some bolts for the nuts."

"Isn't it called a screw?" she said.

And in my great fatherly wisdom I replied, "No, you screw the nut on the bolt, but it's called a bolt and not a screw."

"OK, Daddy," Alyssa said, "I don't have enough cell phone minutes for this, so I'd better go."

Communication is not easy. James gave us this clear picture: "No one can tame the tongue" (James 3:8 NCV). We live in a nation where 50 percent of wives say husbands don't communicate, 86 percent of those divorced say the cause was deficient communication, and 25 percent of young people indicate they have never had one meaningful conversation with their father. We need help!

Our words have the power to take our relationships to a new level of impact and intimacy.

When you get right down to it, communication is not a science; it is an art. It's not black and white. It's not always logical, and you certainly cannot reduce successful communication to a simple equation. Communication is an art, filled with fine lines and shades of meaning. As communication artists, most of us are still stuck in kindergarten, struggling with little fingers to learn to grasp a fat crayon so we can at least color between the lines.

We need an expert to teach us—someone who can paint a communication masterpiece. Who better to turn to than the *only* perfect communicator who ever walked this earth—Jesus Christ?

Jesus has some wonderful—but also some unsettling— things to teach us about communication. We learn from not only his words but also his example. He taught about communication through the way he spoke to people—whether a struggling sinner or a proud Pharisee. We often think of Jesus' communication skills in terms of his sermons to the great crowds, yet Jesus was just as good a communicator to the individual.

As a part of my study of how Jesus related to people, I read through the Gospels with one question in mind: "How did Jesus communicate?" I began to pick up on three lessons about communication that grow out of the teaching and example of Jesus—lessons we'll examine in more depth for the next three days: (1) the foundation of communication is trust; (2) communication is always from the heart; and (3) communication that makes an impact is honest. Frankly, I didn't find any of these lessons to be comforting at first. Instead, each held unexpected surprises and unwelcome challenges. What started as a walk down the garden path of truth very quickly began to feel more like a bobsled run toward honesty! The example of Jesus shows us that our words have the power to take our relationships to a new level of impact and intimacy.

EXPERIENCE THE TRUTH

Jesus sat quietly with the little girl and said two words that changed everything. His journey to be with her had been filled with twists and turns. The little girl was ill, and so her father had come to Jesus for help. This dad was also an important government official. He knew how to get things done, and yet he can see that his daughter is gravely ill, and nothing is working to get her well. So the official, Jairus by name, turns to Jesus for help. He seeks out Jesus in the busy marketplace and secures his agreement to come and help his daughter.

Picture Jairus, stone-faced with anxiety, dividing the crowd as he rushes back toward his home so that Jesus and his disciples can follow in his wake. They're making good progress when Jesus suddenly stops. "Who touched me," he says. Even Jesus' disciples are incredulous. In this kind of crowd, everyone is constantly bumping against each other. If the disciples are shocked, Jairus must have felt pure panic. Every second counted—didn't Jesus know that? But Jesus takes a few moments to deal with a woman who had been suffering for twelve years and whose life is suddenly changed by her trust that touching Jesus will heal her.

The group continues its press through the crowd. When they arrive at Jairus's home, they are greeted by the sound of weeping. The community has already gathered to weep with this family, because the little girl has died. Jesus speaks before Jairus has a chance to plead, "Why didn't you get here more quickly? Why did you have to stop?" "She's not dead; she's just asleep," Jesus says. The people gathered laugh at Jesus. In that society many mourners would be there with the family, even though they weren't close to the family—and their tears turn quickly to laughter.

Jesus walks past their sarcastic smiles to the room

where the little girl is lying. He takes her by the hand, bends down, and whispers two simple words into her ear: *"Talitha koum!"** Talitha koum —* "Little girl, get up."

And so the little girl stands up, and Jesus asks her parents to get her something to eat.

Based on Mark 5:22 – 43

Two words, and then a miracle. If you think God cannot work a miracle through your words, then you've missed the point of the power of God. While you may not be given the ability to heal someone physically with your words, there is no doubt that your words can heal a relationship, heal someone's faith, heal a broken heart, heal a shattered hope.

---

*Most Bible translations retain these two words in the original Aramaic language because you can hear the tender heart of Jesus in the sound of these words, even before knowing what they mean.

Principle #3: Communicate from the Heart

Thinking about My Relationships

Point to Ponder: All relationships are fueled by communication.

Verse to Remember: *Reckless words pierce like a sword, but the tongue of the wise brings healing* (Proverbs 12:18).

Question to Consider: Who needs to hear me speak words that heal?

Tomorrow: The foundation is trust

16

The Foundation
Is Trust

The foundation of communication is trust. In his Sermon on the Mount, Jesus said, "Simply let your 'Yes' be 'Yes,' and your 'No,' 'No'; anything beyond this comes from the evil one" (Matthew 5:37). Jesus tells us that we must say what we mean and mean what we say. You cannot have high-quality communication without high-level trust. With great trust there can be great communication. With little trust there is little communication, and with no trust there is no communication. If I cannot trust what you say, it really doesn't matter how great the words or how fervent the plea. Whether we're working at establishing a relationship or rebuilding channels of communication, *it has to begin with trust.*

At a sixth grade school camp I attended with my son Luke, the counselors involved the kids in games to get them to start talking. One of the games targeted this issue of trust. "Tell us three facts about yourself," the counselor said to the circle of on-the-verge adolescents. "Two of the facts need to be a lie, and one of the facts needs to be true." It was somewhat refreshing to find out that these sixth graders were *not* very good at this game. They would say things like, "I'm seven feet tall, I weigh five hundred pounds, and I like basketball." Unfortunately, most adults would be a lot better at it!

The question the game prompted in my mind was this: "How many lies does it take to stop trusting someone?" *One* is all that is needed. Introduce one lie into a relationship, and trust is eroded. We cannot have high-quality communication without high-level trust.

Communication experts say that the words we speak to others can actually produce six distinct messages:

- what you mean to say
- what you actually say
- what the other person hears
- what the other person thinks he hears
- what the other person says about what you said
- what you think the other person said about what you said*

What do you think happens when you mix even a little dishonesty, a few lies, into what is already a difficult endeavor? You turn communication into a total mess.

Jesus speaks to us about the center of this trust with utter simplicity: "Let your 'Yes' be 'Yes,' and your 'No,' 'No.'" Trust is centered on two tiny words — *Yes* and *No*. How we choose to use these words becomes the factory where trust is assembled.

Every parent understands the power of these two simple words and how deeply they affect our trust. Suppose a six-

---

*See H. Norman Wright, *Communication: Key to Your Marriage* (Ventura, Calif.: Regal, 1974), 54.

year-old son runs to his father when he gets home and says, "Can we go to the park tonight, Daddy?" When Dad says, "Sure, son," the little boy hears a yes loudly and clearly. If that yes is later changed to a no, no matter how good the reason, trust suffers a blow and communication is hurt.

If I could choose one place to be perfect, it would be in my parenting. Every word, every action, has an impact on my children—often in ways I don't see or understand. Yet just as I did not have perfect parents, my children do not have perfect parents. There are so many things that can go wrong, so many decisions to make, so many little moments that can either be captured or ignored. It's refreshing to hear from Jesus a simple formula for using our words to build trust: watch carefully how you use the words *yes* and *no*.

Eroding Trust

Often without even intending to, we use words in ways that erode trust in our relationships. Take a moment to ask yourself if you are eroding trust in one of these four very familiar ways:

1. Lies

Lies are always told in the absence of trust.

The next time you're challenging one of your kids on whether they've told the truth and they look up at you with those big "you don't think I'd lie to you, do you?" eyes, what are you going to say? "No, of course not; I would never think such a thing"?

Here's a suggestion from John Ortberg on what you might want to say:

"Do I think you'd lie? Of course I do.

"I lie. Your mom lies, that's for sure. Everybody I've ever known has lied. The most famous story about lying in American history is the story of George Washington cutting down a cherry tree. His father asked him who did it. George is supposed to have said, 'I cannot tell a lie; it was me.' That was in a biography written by Parson Weems in the nineteenth century—he made the story up. The most famous story about not lying in America was a lie.

"Anybody who says he or she never lies is lying. Mostly I think you tell the truth, but absolutely I think you'd lie."*

2. Flattery

Flattery is just a positive lie designed to increase your standing in another person's eyes. Because flattery uses others' need for acceptance against them, it is a heartlessly manipulative lie. We're not talking about looking for the best in others and finding a way to encourage them—that's not flattery. Flattery is a flat-out lie about someone's skills or actions for the purposes of personal gain. "What's the problem with a little flattery?" you may ask. It's this: Flattery involves telling lies—lies that hurt others for your gain. Flattery invites someone to believe something about himself that isn't true, and if he does believe it, his life can easily be sent spinning in the wrong direction. Solomon declared, "Liars hate the people they hurt, and false praise can ruin others" (Proverbs 26:28 NCV). William Penn wrote, "Avoid flatterers,

---

*John Ortberg, *When the Game Is Over, It All Goes Back in the Box* (Grand Rapids: Zondervan, 2007), 113.

for they are thieves in disguise."* The Greek philosopher
Antisthenes is reported to have said, "It is better to fall among
crows than among flatterers; for those only devour the dead,
these the living."†

3. Broken Promises

I was talking to my friend Tom Vegh, former head of a
successful Christian music company, about the unique
challenges of working with Christians. It surprised me to
hear him say that one of the greatest challenges is broken
promises. Believers sign a contract, but then they ask to get
out of the agreement by saying something like, "God is telling
me to go in a different direction." It's all too easy to use God
as an excuse for a broken promise. Jesus, God in human flesh,
told us to let our "Yes" be "Yes"; in fact, he said that when we
go beyond this simple affirmation of the truth to manipulate
words in an effort to get our own way, we're being ruled by
the evil one (see Matthew 5:37).

4. Silence

Silence is another way in which we can erode trust—and
this is certainly an area of struggle for me. I thought I was a
good communicator when my wife and I were first married.
I worked really hard at listening well. One day, Chaundel
informed me that, while my listening skills were improving,
communication also involved my *talking* to her. This was
earth-shattering, shocking news! Whenever I would stay

---

*William Penn, "Letter to His Wife and Children," August 4, 1682.
†Quoted in Diogenes Laertius, *The Lives and Opinions of Eminent Philosophers*,
trans. C. D. Yonge (London: Henry G. Bohn, 1853).

silent, she was left wondering what I was thinking, which certainly doesn't build trust.

You cannot have high-quality communication without high-level trust. What if the trust is no longer there? How do you rebuild trust after you've told a lie, chosen to use flattering words, broken a promise, or hidden behind a veil of silence? Rebuilding trust always takes a combination of truth plus time. Building a foundation of trust is hard work, and *re*building a foundation of trust is even harder. Years ago, my in-laws went to San Francisco to help rebuild houses whose foundations had been damaged by an earthquake. The crews actually had to put huge timbers under the houses, lift them with a crane, rebuild the foundations while the houses were up in the air, and then set them back down on a strong foundation.

> *Rebuilding trust always takes a combination of truth plus time.*

As you read this, I hope you'll commit to rebuilding trust with a friend, a son, a daughter, a husband, a wife. As you make this commitment, a healthy dose of honesty will help you as you face the future. Here's the reality: it will *not* be easy. It will take time. Like those San Francisco houses, at times you'll feel stuck in the air without a foundation — and when you do, you may find that connecting with a pastor or a Christian counselor can be helpful in giving you an outside perspective to make it through the difficult rebuilding time. But through it all, know this: even though it will be difficult, once you've rebuilt and set your relationship down again on a foundation of trust, it will have been worth it all. The relationship is worth saving.

As you're building or rebuilding trust, don't forget this simple truth from the Bible: "Kind words are good medicine" (Proverbs 15:4 CEV). The power of a kind word at the right moment is immeasurable!

Just think of the trust that will be built or rebuilt in our relationships if we get better at using these two simple words (*yes* and *no*) in conversations. The applications are almost endless:

- Yes, I love you.
- No, I wasn't listening.
- Yes, I respect you.
- No, I never realized how much I'd hurt you.
- Yes, I'll keep my promise to take you to the park.
- No, throwing a tantrum won't make me give in to you. (You can apply this one to a five-year-old or a fifty-year-old!)
- Yes, I enjoy being with you.
- No, I can't accept what you are doing
- Yes, I'll go through this with you.

The foundation of communication is trust. And Jesus teaches us that trust begins with the way in which we use the words *yes* and *no*.

DAY SIXTEEN

Thinking about My Relationships

Point to Ponder: You cannot have high-level communication without high-level trust.

Verse to Remember: *"Simply let your 'Yes' be 'Yes,' and your 'No,' 'No'; anything beyond this comes from the evil one"* (Matthew 5:37).

Question to Consider: Is the way in which I'm using my words eroding trust or building trust?

Tomorrow: The connection between mouth and heart

17

The Connection between Mouth and Heart

I feel uncomfortably challenged by what Jesus taught about the connection between our mouths and our hearts. You see, I'm a real believer in the accidental "slip of the tongue." When I say something that earns an unexpected and unpleasant reaction, I'd rather say, "I didn't really mean it," than face the relational consequences. Now if you think this means I'm a coward at times—you're absolutely right!

Jesus said, "Out of the overflow of the heart the mouth speaks" (Matthew 12:34). Ouch! Jesus speaks of a direct link between the mouth and the heart. Your foot pushes the accelerator of a car, and the speed increases—a direct connection. Your finger pokes the "up" button outside the elevator, and the doors swish open—a direct connection. Your heart is feeling bitter, and your words become sarcastic —also a direct connection. I'd like to think I can avoid this connection, somehow cut off the overflow before it actually spills out. *Our* solution is often, "If I could just build a bigger dam, nothing will overflow." So we dam up our emotions, our fears, our hearts. Eventually, of course, the dam bursts—and what should have been a refreshing stream of honesty becomes a destructive flood of pent-up words.

Now for the clincher. The connection between the mouth and heart is actually a *two-way* connection. My heart affects the words that come out of my mouth, *and* the words that come out of my mouth affect my heart. Notice what Jesus taught in Mark 7:15 (LB): "Your souls aren't harmed by what you eat, but by what you think and say!" This reciprocal connection causes us to sometimes get caught up in a vicious circle of words. The anger in our heart spills out in biting words that magnify the anger inside and wound our soul. The wounded soul reacts by striking out with more angry words.

As a picture of this reciprocal connection, I'm reminded of an older gentleman who was running around the track at a high school. Football practice was going on in the middle of the field, and the high school boys were doing wind sprints. The older man thought to himself, "As long as those boys are sprinting, I think I'll keep jogging." But he went around the track time after time, and the boys kept sprinting. Finally, reaching the point where he needed to go home, the man stopped. The boys also stopped and headed for the locker room. As one of the boys passed by, he said to the older man, "Sir, I'm really glad you finally stopped jogging. Coach told us, 'As long as that old man can jog, you young guys can surely keep sprinting!'"

Words designed to hurt others hurt you the most deeply of all.

Can you see places in which you are caught in a vicious circle of words? At work, at home, with friends? The question is, "How do you break the pattern?" The answer isn't found in trying to break this inevitable connection between what's in your heart and what you say. When you think about what Jesus teaches, you realize this is a battle that can only be won when fought on two fronts—the heart and the mouth. Since words are an overflow of the heart, start taking your *heart* more seriously. Instead of pretending that your words meant nothing, ask yourself why you said what you said. And since our souls are harmed by what we say, start taking your *words* more seriously. Realize that words designed to hurt others hurt you the most deeply of all.

There is no arena of life that is immune from the dangers of this vicious circle of words. I sometimes hear people excuse their ugly words in areas such as theology or politics. The assumption is that those on different sides of an issue can say whatever they want to gain an advantage with no qualms about igniting a battle that ends up wounding everyone. This is simply a lie that we tell ourselves. Theologians who speak rancorous words stir up trouble in their hearts and in the hearts of those they hope to teach. Politicians who speak viciously in national debates deepen anger in their hearts and in the heart of a listening nation. As one who loves the lessons taught in history, I'm reminded of the famous division and reconciliation that occurred between Thomas Jefferson and John Adams—two men who had become friends in the forging of American independence. But their sharply divergent views on governing the new nation turned them into political enemies and then personal enemies. It wasn't until later in life that a mutual friend encouraged them to restore their relationship, which they did through the writing of the Adams–Jefferson letters so treasured by historians today. As it turned out, these two reconciled friends died in their separate homes on the same day, July 4, 1826; the fiftieth anniversary of their signing of the Declaration of Independence. How different the story would have been for them personally and for their influence on others if they had never reconciled!

Let's boil these truths down to actions we can take in our everyday lives. Have you ever tried to refocus your emotions in the middle of an argument? To intentionally calm yourself in the heat of battle? I hope you have, because then you'll know how difficult it is, and you won't take these next thoughts lightly. There is no instant formula for success. It's certainly not like flipping a light switch from off to on. Your emotions are engaged; patterns of how you've communicated in the past are involved, as well as past hurts and frustrations. It's even possible hunger — and the resulting low blood sugar — is involved. (Ever notice that the worst family arguments are often right before a meal?)

Here are a few strategies that can help break the cycle before the words start pouring out of your mouth:

- Take five ... or ten! Get away for ten minutes, and let your anger cool down.
- Pray for the other person.
- Wait until *after* you've eaten to have the difficult conversation.
- Use owning statements instead of blaming statements — don't blame the other person for your feelings; own them yourself.
- Watch the tone and the volume of your words.
- Focus on the solution, not the problem.
- Learn to accept what cannot be changed.

While these simple strategies can help to break the circle of hurtful words, you need to take a deeper step. You must change the focus of your heart—and Jesus tells you how to do it. Jesus often taught about a broad reality that points the way to a change of heart. At first, his teaching may sound too theological to have anything to do with everyday relationships. I'm talking about Jesus' teaching on the kingdom of God. He showed us that the kingdom is the key to heart change: "Change your hearts and lives, because the kingdom of heaven is near" (Matthew 4:17 NCV). The truth of God's kingdom is at the core of dealing with our selfish hearts: "He will give you all you need from day to day if you live for him and make the Kingdom of God your primary concern" (Matthew 6:33 NLT).

The truth of God's kingdom is at the core of dealing with our selfish hearts.

Suppose you're sitting on a bus holding a book that has the words *Kingdom of God* in the title. The person sitting across from you sees the book and says, "The kingdom of God—I've always wanted to know what the kingdom of God is." What would you say? One answer—one you'd be able to share before the bus comes to its next stop—is, "God's kingdom is where God is recognized as King." In the prayer Jesus taught us, we pray, "Your kingdom come, your will be done" (Matthew 6:10). God's kingdom is where God's will is done.

How does this truth from the Bible fit with our patterns of communication? In any conversation, someone is wearing the crown—it could be you, trying desperately to get your way, or it could be the other person. The truth is, it's often both who are striving to gain control. The only path to a change of heart is to take off the fake and paltry crown you've fashioned for yourself. Your heart changes whenever and wherever you recognize that God is the *only* rightful wearer of the crown. *He is the only King.* I've found it helpful to visualize myself taking the crown off and praying, "God, you are the only one wearing a crown in this conversation." Recognizing God's kingship and not ours has the power to break a pattern characterized by vicious words and to begin a new pattern characterized by life-giving words.

DAY SEVENTEEN
Thinking about My Relationships

Point to Ponder: There is a two-way connection between my mouth and my heart.

Verse to Remember: *"Change your hearts and lives, because the kingdom of heaven is near"* (Matthew 4:17 NCV).

Questions to Consider: Am I caught up in a vicious circle of words with someone? What steps do I need to take to break the pattern?

Tomorrow: A new kind of honesty

18

A New Kind of Honesty

Groucho Marx once said, "The secret of life is honesty and fair dealing. If you can fake that, you've got it made." That's funny because it reveals our universal struggle with honesty. Most of us value honesty; we want honesty to be a part of our lives and relationships. Yet when it comes right down to it, we often find it easier to be dishonest. Whether a "little white lie" or a blatantly selfish deceit, we cave in to dishonesty because we'd rather not give the conversational time and energy it would take to be honest. Suppose you're having a problem with a friend at work. He or she walks by your desk and says, "How are you doing today?" At that moment you have a choice. You can say, "Fine," and the conversation is over. No time, no energy, no potential misunderstanding or blowup. Or you could choose to be honest: "Actually, there's something I've been meaning to talk to you about. Do you have a few minutes at lunch?"

Here are a few of the honesty questions all of us must face: How many times last week did I give the "fine" answer?

How many times did it just seem easier to not be honest? How many times did staying silent leave a relationship where it was when a moment of honesty could have deepened the relationship?

As I read through each conversation of Jesus and asked myself what I could learn about communication, the most striking lesson for me came in these two words: *Be honest.* Jesus' conversations have a different kind of honesty than most of us ever practice or experience. Because Jesus wasn't constrained by others' opinions of him and his love wasn't stained by selfishness, Jesus is refreshingly, strikingly, wonderfully *honest.*

Because he is honest, Jesus' words are often surprising. He commends an enemy of his people for his "great faith" (Matthew 8:8–10), and he rebukes his own disciple Peter for his "little faith" (Matthew 14:28–31). He calls the Pharisees hypocrites and snakes (Matthew 23:29, 33), and then he prays, "Father, forgive them" (Luke 23:34). He rebuked his friends sternly, yet he taught them compassionately and loved them sacrificially.

EXPERIENCE THE TRUTH

Jesus and his followers are warming themselves by a fire and talking about the future. The conversation is not going as the disciples had hoped. In the back of each of their minds, there have been growing thoughts of glory. As they've watched the miracles of Jesus and listened to his words, these men have become more and more convinced that he is the leader their nation has been waiting for. Jesus is headed for national glory, and they are going with him. He is the king they've been looking for, and they will rule with him.

But Jesus isn't talking about ruling; he is talking about suffering, about dying. And every one of those men felt deeply uncomfortable with what Jesus was saying. It didn't fit their image of what should happen — it just felt wrong.

Peter is the one who finally said it. Someone needed to set Jesus straight, and Peter was just the one to do it! So he called Jesus off to the side. "Never, Lord," Peter said in a passionate whisper, just loud enough for the others to hear. "All this talk of dying — it's just *not* going to happen to you."

Jesus turned to look Peter straight in the eye. In the brief pause before he spoke, it was obvious this was a supremely dramatic moment. Jesus uttered these unforgettably honest words: "Get behind me, Satan! You are a stumbling block to me. You do not have in mind the concerns of God, but merely human concerns."

Based on Matthew 16:21 - 23

Wow! It's hard to imagine a more scathing reply.

As I studied the conversations of Jesus, I have to admit that more than once I felt a little uncomfortable. His words at times seemed harsh. He certainly didn't appear to be overly concerned about protecting others' feelings. This conversation with Peter stands as one of the starkest examples. Then I thought, "If there is a difference between the way that seems right to me and the example that Jesus gives — which should win out?" Should I listen more to *my* feelings and opinions on the subject, or should I pay greatest attention to the example of the Master of the universe and the Lord of life?

As I reflected on the words of Jesus, I realized that it's a lot easier for me to be nice than to be honest. Honesty is a lot more work. It is the work of thinking through the right way to say something, of making sure my motives are pure, of talking through a difficult subject. It is the reality of facing my own anxieties — a beating heart and sweaty palms — when I take the risk to be honest.

But if we want our relationships to grow, honesty is nonnegotiable. When we are honest, we will always be "speaking the truth in love" (Ephesians 4:15). Look at the word *truth* in that verse, and look also at *love*. It takes both — truth wrapped in love.

Truth without love doesn't work. Some people use the truth like a weapon. They don't tell the truth; they *aim* it. The truth sometimes hurts, but it doesn't have to maim, kill, or destroy. As Paul urges, "Do not let any unwholesome talk come out of your mouths, but only what is helpful for building others up according to their needs" (Ephesians 4:29).

On the other hand, love without truth is equally disastrous. Apart from honesty, any relationship will suffer from a lack of trust — and this lack of trust will cause great pain. It may be the loud pain of constant arguments or the quiet hurt of silence — but it will be painful. Apart from truth, trust will erode.

One of my greatest mistakes in the early years of marriage was not being honest with Chaundel about my sexual temptations as a man. It just seemed like the "nice" thing to do — after all, I wanted her to know that she was the most beautiful woman in the world to me. And to be more candid, it was the easier thing to do. Any man who has tried to explain his temptations to a woman — with the amazingly different wiring of men and women — knows that it means a long, intense conversation. It may have seemed nicer and easier, but it was exactly the wrong thing to do. My wife is no dummy! She knew that I faced temptations. My reticence to talk didn't reassure her of her place in my life; it only made her wonder if there was a reason to not trust me. It was only as I finally decided to speak the truth in love that we were able to have honest conversations that led to a deeper relationship. And I have to tell you, waiting to have this conversation didn't make it any easier. Here's a little free advice: When you know you need to have an honest conversation, have it *now*. It will never be any easier to have that conversation, and all of us have experienced the painful reality that waiting usually makes it much more difficult.

> Truth without love doesn't work. Love without truth is equally disastrous.

A man who was at the top of his game once approached Jesus, wanting to learn what it meant to follow Jesus. He is described as a rich young ruler. Think of the influence he could have on others — and he was interested in following Jesus! The disciples had to be salivating at the prospect of such an important man becoming one of their supporters.

While we might have been tempted to make the truth as palatable as possible for this powerful man, Jesus is content to simply be honest. "Good teacher," the man says, and Jesus replies, "Why do you call me good? No one is good—except God alone" (Luke 18:18–19). Fancy words of flattery were immediately off-limits in this conversation. As they talk about God's commandments, the ruler says, "All these I've kept since I was a boy." Jesus honestly tells him, "You still lack one thing. Sell everything you have and give to the poor" (Luke 18:21–22). During his ministry, Jesus didn't challenge any other person to sell everything before following him. This was the honest truth that this particular man at this particular time needed to hear.

The truth forces a momentous decision: accept or reject. This man rejected the truth. He walked away, shoulders slumping with sadness. Jesus did not chase after him. Even though his own disciples were left asking, "If *this* man couldn't be saved, who then can be saved?" Jesus allowed the man to make the honest choice to say no.

If you communicate honestly, you *will* be rejected. Jesus himself—the one perfect human being—was rejected. Honesty sometimes brings the bitter pain of rejection. But it can also bring the amazing joy of acceptance. As you communicate honestly, you *will* invite yourself and others to refreshing life change through your words. Honesty is not for the faint of heart, because it is a risk—a risk well worth taking to open yourself up to a remarkable potential for change.

Thinking about My Relationships

Point to Ponder: It is easier to be nice than to be honest.

Verse to Remember: *Speaking the truth in love, we will in all things grow up into him who is the Head, that is, Christ* (Ephesians 4:15).

Question to Consider: Is there someone with whom I need to take the risk to have an honest conversation?

Tomorrow: God is in the conversation

19

God Is
in the Conversation

One of the most vital aspects of your communication with people is prayer. More important than the way you talk to someone is the way you talk to God about them. The way you talk to God about the people in your life will determine such things as your ability to let go of a hurt, the eyes of faith through which you look at the future, and the wisdom you have as you make decisions. Yet prayer is not always seen as such a powerful change agent. The experience of many is that prayer seems boring and routine, an exercise reserved for bedtimes and bad times.

Prayer is like driving. Everyone thinks they're good at it—until they're in the presence of an expert. When Jesus' disciples heard him pray, everything changed. Prayer probably hadn't meant much to them; they saw it as the domain of religious men in fancy dress on street corners and of paid representatives at funerals. Prayer was a show, a kind of a spiritual medal to be worn proudly and openly. Then along came Jesus. He'd get up early to pray when faced with the busiest of days (Mark 1:35). He prayed a prayer of thanks over a few loaves and fish, and five thousand men were fed (Mark 6:41). He went to a mountain to pray and was met there by Moses and Elijah (Luke 9:28). Having seen all this, the disciples followed Jesus one day and stood in hushed respect as their Master prayed on a hillside. They knew who he was talking to, and so they wouldn't think of interrupting. But when Jesus was done, one of them made the request that was on everyone's mind: "Lord, teach us to pray" (Luke 11:1). Class was in session.

While there is so much to say about prayer, I want to focus here on how Jesus treated prayer as a relationship. Many common misconceptions about prayer can easily creep into our thinking. Some view prayer as a magic wand; wave it correctly and get whatever you want. Others see prayer as just a first-aid kit—something to break into "only in case of an emergency." For some, prayer is a last resort; for others, it's a tug-of-war—a game played with God to convince him to do something. And many who would accept none of these other false concepts of prayer struggle with the most dangerous lie of all, namely, that prayer is simply a duty. "I should pray more," they say, "but my heart just isn't in it."

> More important than the way you talk to someone is the way you talk to God about them.

Jesus taught us that prayer is a conversation. Now that's refreshing! Let's go a step further and ask, "What kind of a conversation? What can we learn from Jesus about the way in which we are to talk with God?" In Jesus' example and teaching, three words mark the tone of our conversation with God: *persistence, confidence,* and *reverence.*

Persistence

Jesus tells a number of parables about persistence in which he reminds his followers that "they should always pray and not give up" (Luke 18:1; see also Luke 11:5–13). These stories are frequently misunderstood. At first reading, it appears that God is like a judge who has to be persuaded to listen to a widow, or like a friend who has to be talked into loaning a friend some food. It's important to realize that parables can be either a parable of comparison (God is like ...) or of contrast (God is the exact opposite of ...), and these two parables are parables of contrast. God is exactly the opposite of the friend and the judge who were reluctant to help. God loves to give willingly and freely. The point of the stories is this: if these unwilling people were persuaded by someone's persistence, how much more can you count on a loving and willing God to answer your requests when you persist in prayer. It was the accepted practice in that day to pray no more than three times a day so God wouldn't get tired of hearing you. Jesus shatters this concept by showing that we should always pray and not give up (see Luke 18:1).

God doesn't have to be coaxed or pressured into helping. You don't have to nag him. Your persistence is instead an indicator of your desire and your dependence on God. Unless you truly depend on God, you will not persist in the conversation. You will make a request at God's customer service counter and click on the stopwatch. If God doesn't come through in your prescribed time frame, you'll try another way. Persistence in prayer is born of knowing that the answer is *only* with God.

People frequently ask, "How long should I keep praying

about this situation?" Pray until one of two things happens: God changes the situation, or God changes you. Often both will happen at once. And while you're waiting, realize that God is working. We're in a hurry, but God is not. He can afford to take the long view in his answers to our prayers. Martin Luther once said, "Prayer is not overcoming God's reluctance. It is laying hold of God's willingness."[*]

Confidence

Jesus taught that part of the conversation in prayer is making confident requests of God. "Ask and it will be given to you; seek and you will find; knock and the door will be opened to you," said Jesus (Matthew 7:7). One of reasons we don't ask, seek, and knock is because we lack confidence. Jesus does his best to remedy this:

> "Everyone who asks receives; he who seeks finds; and to him who knocks, the door will be opened.
> "Which of you, if his son asks for bread, will give him a stone? Or if he asks for a fish, will give him a snake? If you, then, though you are evil, know how to give good gifts to your children, how much more will your Father in heaven give good gifts to those who ask him!"
>
> Matthew 7:8-11

Pray with the expectation that something will happen — or why bother to pray at all? This issue deserves deeper reflection. Perhaps we don't feel confident when we pray

---

[*]Quoted in D. A. Carson, *For the Love of God*, vol. 2 (Wheaton, Ill.: Crossway, 2006), 18.

because of the times we've made specific requests and no answer was forthcoming: "God didn't heal"; "my friend wasn't saved"; or (forgive me, Lord, for my pettiness) "I didn't find my lost car keys." These experiences cause us to think, "Maybe my conversation with God shouldn't contain requests. Maybe it should just be an expression of praise and a time of listening to God." Nice thought, but it isn't what Jesus taught. Jesus put it quite simply: "Ask."

As you ask, remember that it is not your job to protect God's reputation. Some stop asking because they feel embarrassed for God when the answers don't come at the exactly the time or in the manner in which we would like them to come. The answers are up to God. Jesus taught that *our job is to pray with confidence.*

Picture the four-year-old daughter of a single mother asking one day, "Mommy, can I go to college?" "Yes," says the mom—with a gulp. That

> God is answering many of your prayers in ways you can't yet see.

very day the mom begins to save a little each day for college. Her commitment involves giving up a daily latte at the local coffeehouse and carefully planning meals. While the four-year-old can't understand it yet, her request is already being answered. Likewise, God is answering many of your prayers in ways you can't yet see—in ways you may not see until you get to heaven. To acknowledge this doesn't provide an excuse; it recognizes our limitations and expresses confidence in God's perfect plan and power.

Of course our confidence must be an *informed* confidence —a confidence that wouldn't pray, as an obvious example, that God would strike someone dead, because we know that

God declares, "You shall not murder" (Exodus 20:13). The exciting truth is, the better you know the will of God revealed in the Bible, the more confidently you can pray.

What should be a confident conversation with God often turns into timid talk. Jesus makes it clear: "Ask!" "What if I ask for the wrong thing or ask in the wrong way?" you may wonder. God will let you know. Give him a good, honest request to work with, and he can clearly answer it or clearly reject it.

Reverence

The most radical thing Jesus taught us about the conversation of prayer is contained in the first line of the Lord's Prayer: "Our Father in heaven" (Matthew 6:9). Jesus taught us to begin our prayers with an expression of reverence. True awe is not found in considering God as distant and untouchable. Jesus taught us to reverently call God "our Father." Prayer is a relationship. Some people see prayer as something like a government tax form on which all the boxes must be correctly filled in to get a quick refund. The right "thee" in this box, the right "thou" in that box, the right "O most benevolent heavenly ruler" at the top, and the right "in Jesus' name. Amen," at the bottom. Reverence in prayer isn't about methods and forms — it's a relationship.

In Jesus' day, no one would have dared to use the term *Father* in addressing God. Jesus taught us to pray in a new way: "Our Father in heaven." Each word challenges us to question seriously the kind of relationship we have with God:

- *Our* invites us to ask, "How *small* is my God?" Some

people have a God so small that he can only fit into their little world. He can only meet their individual needs. Notice that there is no *I* or *me* in the Lord's Prayer, it's all *our* and *us*.

- *Father* brings to the surface the question, "How *close* is my God?" — "as close as a loving father," Jesus showed. The closer we get to God, the closer we get to real life.
- *In heaven* induces the question, "How *big* is my God?" "In heaven" doesn't mean someplace far away; it points to the eternal place of power and control. As God's children, we have instant access to our powerful Father.

For Jesus, conversation with his Father was a part of the fabric of his life. He prayed through all hours of the night and early in the morning. He prayed alone, with his disciples, and in front of crowds. He prayed lengthy and focused prayers, and he also interrupted a teaching or conversation to offer a brief prayer. Jesus prayed in the comfort of time alone with his Father in the hills of Galilee, in the pressure of a time of decision in the garden of Gethsemane, and in the torture of his time of suffering on the cross at Calvary. He prayed when someone needed to be fed and when someone needed to be healed. He prayed when parents asked for their children to be blessed. He prayed when there was a person to be forgiven.

For Jesus, prayer was simply a conversation with his Father in heaven. He taught us to have the same kind of conversation — a conversation marked by persistence, confidence, and reverence.

As this chapter concludes, I invite you to join me in this prayer:

Jesus, teach me to pray. I want prayer to be a part of the fabric of my life. Yet all too often I feel so far from that kind of conversation with God. Instead of focusing on what I lack, help me to focus in faith on what you offer to me, Jesus. Teach me to pray. Amen.

DAY NINETEEN
Thinking about My Relationships

Point to Ponder: For Jesus, prayer was simply a conversation with his Father in heaven.

Verses to Remember: *"This, then, is how you should pray: 'Our Father in heaven, hallowed be your name, your kingdom come, your will be done on earth as it is in heaven. Give us today our daily bread. Forgive us our debts, as we also have forgiven our debtors. And lead us not into temptation, but deliver us from the evil one'"* (Matthew 6:9–13).

Question to Consider: How could patience, confidence, and reverence become a greater part of my conversation with God this week?

Tomorrow: How to be truly heard

20

How to Be
Truly Heard

Build trust, watch your heart, and be honest—as we learned
on Days 16, 17, and 18, this is Jesus' prescription for great
communication. Alongside these three commitments, we
discover other truths from the way in which Jesus talked
to people. Jesus showed us how to make an impact with our
words. He taught us how to move beyond merely speaking
words to being truly heard. We see Jesus strengthening his
communication again and again in three powerful ways:
giving a gentle touch, asking the right question, and painting
pictures with his words.

Jesus Touched Those He Healed

Jesus often touched those he healed. Consider these two
examples from the gospel of Luke:

> As the sun went down that evening, all the villagers who
> had any sick people in their homes, no matter what their

diseases were, brought them to Jesus; and the touch of his hands healed every one!

Luke 4:40 LB

"Sir," [the man with leprosy] said, "if only you will, you can clear me of every trace of my disease."

Jesus reached out and touched the man and said, "Of course I will. Be healed." And the leprosy left him instantly!

Luke 5:12–13 LB

Why did he touch them? Jesus once healed a man's servant who was several miles away (Matthew 8:5–13), so he obviously didn't have to touch someone in order to heal them.

We can learn from Jesus' example the power of human touch. There is something about a sincere touch on the hand or the shoulder that communicates, "We're in this together." Never underestimate the power of human touch. Rick Warren writes about this in *The Purpose Driven Church*:

Our world is filled with lonely people who are starving for the affirmation of a loving touch....

I recently got this note on a registration card: "Pastor Rick, I can't tell you what it meant to me when you put your arm around me in comfort today. I felt as though Jesus was hugging me in such compassion and tenderness. I now know I will make it through this scary time, and I know he sent you to help me. It's wonderful that there's such caring and love in this church. Thank you." I had no idea when I hugged her she was going in for breast cancer surgery the next day.

Another note from the same week said, "I have been

asking God for a positive sign that he is with me. Before the service, Pastor Glen, whom I've never met, walked by my seat, and without saying a word, put his hand on my shoulder. I know now that the Lord has not forgotten me." The man's wife had left him that week....

> *Jesus taught us how to move beyond merely speaking words to being truly heard.*

You never know how a tender word and a caring touch will make all the difference in the world to someone. Behind every smile is a hidden hurt that a simple expression of love may heal."*

Touch is a powerful method of communication that can be misused or misunderstood. I'm not talking about a phony touch — the kind that feels as though a lizard has just slithered across your arm. I'm talking about a touch of genuine kindness. Jesus had the right touch, because he truly cared about everyone he met.

Jesus Used Questions to Challenge

Jesus often used questions to challenge someone's thinking and to set his or her life in a different direction. Consider these examples:

- Jesus challenged his disciple Peter with the question, "Who do you say I am?" Peter replied, "You are the Messiah" (Mark 8:29 NLT). Jesus' question elicited from

---

*Rick Warren, *The Purpose Driven Church* (Grand Rapids: Zondervan, 1995), 214–15.

Peter's heart one of the greatest statements of faith ever uttered.

- Jesus confronted a blind man with the question, "What do you want me to do for you?" "I want to see," Bartimaeus said (Mark 10:51). And Jesus healed him.
- After Jesus' resurrection, he challenged Peter with a question: "Do you love me more than these others?" "Yes," Peter replied, "you know I am your friend." "Then feed my lambs," Jesus told him (John 21:15 LB). By asking this question, Jesus opened Peter's mind to the calling that would consume him for the rest of his life.

While Jesus often used questions to challenge someone's thinking, we often use volume. If we can't get our point across, we tend to just talk louder. Of course it rarely works; raising the volume tends to push others away. Statements tend to confront and to make us put up barriers. Questions have the ability to challenge and to break down barriers.

Before I became a believer in Jesus in my late teens, some church members knocked on my door to invite me to attend a concert in a nearby park. At one point, the conversation turned to faith in Christ. "Are you a Christian?" someone asked. "I think I'm a Christian," I answered. "Would you like to be sure you are a Christian?" he asked. "No thanks," I stammered and quickly shut the door. The conversation was over, but the question stuck with me. "Could someone really be sure he was a Christian?" I wondered. "Did I have to wait until I faced God in heaven to determine whether I'd been good enough to call myself a Christian?" The seed of the question this person asked me was one of the things that challenged me to think more deeply about Christianity. I discovered that a relationship with God was not dependent on my goodness but on his forgiveness. I found that I needed to repent of my sins and ask God to begin to direct my daily life. One of the reasons I came to this commitment was because this question challenged my thinking.

Jesus Used Pictures
to Communicate New Truth

Do you want to help someone see something they haven't seen before? Paint a picture—because if they're going to really *see* something, they need a picture.

EXPERIENCE THE TRUTH

Two of the most fascinating conversations Jesus had are found in back-to-back chapters early in the gospel of John. The subject of the conversations is the same—what it means to have a relationship with God. Yet the people he spoke to could not have been more opposite.

In John 3 Jesus spoke to Nicodemus—a leader of the community, a man looked up to as a religious and moral example. In John 4 he spoke to a woman by a well in Samaria—a woman so ostracized for her immorality that she had to come alone in the heat of the day to get water rather than with the rest of the city dwellers in the cool of the morning or evening.

Nicodemus intentionally came to speak to Jesus at night because it wouldn't do for a respected leader to be seen with Jesus. The woman at the well accidentally ran into Jesus in the middle of the day. When his disciples found Jesus talking to her, they were shocked that a respected rabbi would take the time to speak with such a woman.

Different people. Different settings. Different needs.

As Jesus spoke to both about what it meant to have a relationship with God, he communicated with pictures to help them understand. To Nicodemus, a religious leader who thought he had it all figured out, Jesus talked about being born again: "With all the earnestness I possess I tell you this: Unless you are born again, you can never get into the Kingdom of God" (John 3:3 LB). To the woman at the well, who knew she had made a mess of her life and relationships, Jesus spoke about the living water that could quench her inner thirst: "If you knew the gift of God and who it is that asks you for a drink, you would have asked him and he would have given you living water" (John 4:10). With these pictures, he helped each of them to see a truth that danced just beyond their grasp.

Based on John 3:1–4:42

The greatest example of Jesus' use of pictures to communicate is seen in his parables. A sheep that had wandered, a coin that was lost, a son who was found (Luke 15), a seed that was scattered, weeds in the field, yeast in the dough (Matthew 13) — in picture after picture Jesus showed us the heart of God. To reopen channels of communication someone has to switch channels. A picture has the power to do this. It has the power to help you see something in a new way.

Jesus teaches us what to do when we feel we are not being heard. Instead of giving up quickly in frustration, try a different way of getting your point across. It's hard work, to be sure. It takes extra effort to offer a healing touch or to phrase just the right question or to paint a picture with your words. But the hard work is worth it, because this extra effort can often point a life or relationship in a completely different direction.

DAY TWENTY
Thinking about My Relationships

Point to Ponder: Take responsibility for helping others hear you.

Verse to Remember: *"Others, like seed sown on good soil, hear the word, accept it, and produce a crop—thirty, sixty or even a hundred times what was sown"* (Mark 4:20).

Questions to Consider: To whom do I need to offer a kind touch of compassion? For whom could a well-phrased question bring a needed challenge? Where do I need to use a picture to communicate a truth I've been having a hard time getting across?

Tomorrow: Troubleshooting communication

Troubleshooting Communication

Before we end our look at Jesus' principle of speaking from the heart, let's once again admit the truth that communication is not easy. What should you do when you run into the inevitable roadblocks, detours, and breakdowns? Most computer manuals have a troubleshooting section, telling you what to do in case something goes wrong. In the example of Jesus, you see clear direction for what to do when things become broken in your communication. Jesus teaches us what we need to know about troubleshooting communication through his response to imperfect people and circumstances that were a regular part of his life.

When Criticized, Jesus Gave a Clear, Confident Response

John records a conversation of Jesus in which he declared to his hearers that he was the light of the world:

Later, in one of his talks, Jesus said to the people, "I am the Light of the world. So if you follow me, you won't be stumbling through the darkness, for living light will flood your path."

The Pharisees replied, "You are boasting—and lying!"

Jesus told them, "These claims are true even though I make them concerning myself. For I know where I came from and where I am going, but you don't know this about me." ...

"Where is your father?" they asked.

Jesus answered, "You don't know who I am, so you don't know who my Father is. If you knew me, then you would know him too."

John 8:12–14, 19 LB

When the Pharisees ask Jesus, "Where is your father?" they are repeating the gossip that Jesus was an illegitimate child. Because Jesus was conceived by the Holy Spirit, it's easy to see how this kind of gossip would have been attractive to those without faith. And the Pharisees were not above a thinly veiled reference to this slur against Jesus and his family.

What are you prone to do when you face the attack of criticism? Attack back? Jesus chose instead to give a clear and confident response. Instead of stooping to the level of his attackers, he told the truth. When you choose to attack in return, it just confirms to the person who criticized you that he or she may be right. Since we're not perfect, there may well be some truth in the criticism. Criticism is like chewing gum—chew on it for a bit to see if there's any flavor of truth, and then spit it out. Give a clear, confident response instead of reacting defensively.

When Honestly Doubted, Jesus Offered Proof

John also records a conversation Jesus had with the disciple Thomas after Jesus had risen from the dead:

> Eight days later the disciples were together again, and this time Thomas was with them. The doors were locked; but suddenly, as before, Jesus was standing among them and greeting them.
>
> Then he said to Thomas, "Put your finger into my hands. Put your hand into my side. Don't be faithless any longer. Believe!"
>
> "My Lord and my God!" Thomas said.
>
> Then Jesus told him, "You believe because you have seen me. But blessed are those who haven't seen me and believe anyway."
>
> John 20:26-29 LB

What should you do when someone doubts your word? First, realize that you're not alone. Jesus himself was doubted, and he always spoke the truth. Whenever you are doubted, you can choose to focus either on yourself or on the other person's need. His or her doubt could be rooted in selfishness, which deserves one kind of response, or in distrust, anger, fear, or insecurity, which deserves an entirely different response.

Jesus focused not on Thomas's doubt but on his need. Jesus could have said, "Who are you to doubt God?" Instead, he humbly invited Thomas to touch the wounds in his hands and side. We'll return to the story of Jesus and Thomas next week when we talk about mercy and judgment.

When Ridiculed,
Jesus Was Silent

The prophet Isaiah received a glimpse of the coming Messiah and shared it in his well-loved chapter 53 of his prophesy. Among other things, Isaiah writes about Jesus as follows:

> He was oppressed and afflicted,
>> yet he did not open his mouth;
> he was led like a lamb to the slaughter,
>> and as a sheep before her shearers is silent,
>> so he did not open his mouth.
>
> Isaiah 53:7

Some comments don't deserve an answer. It's better to just let it go. Criticism should sometimes be answered, but sarcastic or ridiculing criticism is never owed an answer. The Bible tells us that an answer to that brand of criticism will do more harm than good:

> If you reason with an arrogant cynic, you'll get
>> slapped in the face;
>> confront bad behavior and get a kick in the shins.
> So don't waste your time on a scoffer;
>> all you'll get for your pains is abuse.
> But if you correct those who care about life,
>> that's different — they'll love you for it!
>
> Proverbs 9:7-8 MSG

When Backed into a Corner,
Jesus Turned on the Light

Jesus' opponents often tried to back him into a corner when they were talking with him. They would ask a question designed to trap him into saying something for which he could later be condemned. Jesus didn't walk away from those situations. Nor did he walk into the cleverly designed trap. Instead, he turned the light of truth on the situation by offering a different perspective.

Some religious opponents of Jesus once tried to trap him by asking whether taxes should be paid to the emperor Caesar. If Jesus said yes, he would be supporting the oppressive Roman government. If he said no, he would be popular with the people but unlawfully rebelling against Rome. Jesus refused to fall into their either/or way of thinking; instead, he provided a new perspective:

> "Show me the coin used for paying the tax." They brought [Jesus] a denarius, and he asked them, "Whose portrait is this? And whose inscription?"
>
> "Caesar's," they replied.
>
> Then he said to them, "Give to Caesar what is Caesar's, and to God what is God's."
>
> When they heard this, they were amazed. So they left him and went away.
>
> Matthew 22:19-22

When Rejected,
Jesus Went Elsewhere

Perhaps the most difficult and valuable lesson to learn from Jesus is what to do when you or your words are rejected. It's important to realize that even the perfect Son of God was rejected for what he did and said. Don't think rejection is always your fault—at times it certainly is, but not always. Others may reject you and your words even if you do everything right.

So what should you do when you've tried everything and made every effort, only to be rejected? We often do exactly the wrong thing. We are rejected, and we respond by chasing even harder after the person who has rejected us. We think our effort will bring us closer to the person, but it almost always has the opposite effect. Our pursuit makes them feel important. "Wow, someone is chasing after me," they think—and so they reject us even more. It's a game we can never win, yet it's one many parents and children, husbands and wives, and bosses and workers have been playing for years.

Words are the single most important tool given to us by God.

Through his example, Jesus provides the answer. When people asked Jesus to leave, he didn't try to convince them that he should stay; he left, because he knew their hearts were hard. He knew that to pursue them further would only push them further away. Remember that when a rich young man rejected Jesus' offer of faith, Jesus let him walk away (Mark 10:17–30). When a town rejected the message of Jesus, he and his disciples left to go to a different town. This principle is so important that Jesus taught it to his disciples before he sent them out to serve: "If anyone will not welcome you or listen to your words, shake the dust off your feet when you leave that home or town" (Matthew 10:14).

Does this mean you'll never experience a restored relationship with those who have rejected you? Of course not. In reality, the best opportunity for restoration is to stop playing the game of pursuing them for affirmation when they reject you. Draw back from the relationship, stand your ground in a life of faith, and wait for them to move toward you. Find your security in your relationship with God, and realize that you don't need their acceptance in order to be loved and valued. Don't become anxious and start pursuing them again at the first small step they take in your direction. You'll risk being thrown right back into the unhealthy game. Wait to see genuine change, and then build on that change.

Be Courageous

As we conclude our seven-day look at the third relationship principle of Jesus, let me remind you of this truth: *It takes courage to communicate.*

Here is the encouragement: the courage pays off. Words are the single most important tool given to us by God. As Solomon declared, "Death and life are in the power of the tongue" (Proverbs 18:21 NASB). At the Tower of Babel, when God wanted to stop the project, he didn't take away chisels or hammers; he took away the ability to communicate. Words are like bricks—you can use them to smash a window, or you can use them to build a foundation.

Remember the old playground chant "Sticks and stones may break my bones, but words will never hurt me"? It's just not true. Words can break a child's confidence. Words can break a husband's dreams. Words can break a parent's heart. Words can break a wife's joy. Or words can build up and give life. Do you realize the power you possess to strengthen another person with the simple words, "Good job," to heal another by saying, "I'm sorry; please forgive me," or to energize another with the words "I love you"? Think of the times just a few words have had a life-leveraging impact on you. It may have been praise from a football coach or wise words of advice from a grandma or truth from a teacher. Through the words you speak, God has given you more power to build faith, hope, and love into others' lives than you can possibly imagine.

Thinking about My Relationships

Point to Ponder: It takes courage to communicate.

Verse to Remember: *"Death and life are in the power of the tongue"* (Proverbs 18:21 NASB).

Question to Consider: Is there someone who needs to hear you say ...

"I want to begin rebuilding trust"?

"I forgive you"?

"It's been way too long since we've talked"?

"I recognize that my words reveal my heart"?

"Honestly, this is what I want to share with you ..."?

Tomorrow: The danger of judgment

As You Judge, You Will Be Judged

Do not judge, or you too will be judged. For in the same way you judge others, you will be judged, and with the measure you use, it will be measured to you.

Matthew 7:1-2

The Danger
of Judgment

Congratulations! You're over halfway through this forty-day journey toward strengthening your relationships. In the first twenty-one days we looked at three powerful relationship principles modeled and taught by Jesus:

- place the highest value on relationships
- love as Jesus loves you
- communicate from the heart

As we take up the fourth principle, be warned that we face some turbulent waters ahead. This fourth relationship principle—as you judge, you will be judged—grows out of one of the most quoted and most misunderstood of all Jesus' statements:

> "Do not judge, or you too will be judged. For in the same way you judge others, you will be judged, and with the measure you use, it will be measured to you.

Why do you look at the speck of sawdust in your brother's eye and pay no attention to the plank in your own eye? How can you say to your brother, 'Let me take the speck out of your eye,' when all the time there is a plank in your own eye? You hypocrite, first take the plank out of your own eye, and then you will see clearly to remove the speck from your brother's eye."

Matthew 7:1-5

There is a great deal of confusion over these words of Jesus: "Do not judge, or you too will be judged." There is also a great deal of power in what Jesus taught about judgment—teaching that holds the promise of dramatic change for your relationships. These words have the potential to truly revolutionize your marriage. They have the power to make your family life more joyful. Those who take to heart what Jesus teaches about judgment develop a more magnetic personality. They are the kind of people others are drawn to and want to be around; they are the kind of people sought out for advice—because they are seeking to live out Jesus' principle: "Do not judge, or you too will be judged."

My in-laws, Dot and Jimmy Warren, had a profound influence on my life—and on the life of hundreds of others—in large measure because they lived out these words of Jesus. They understood how to offer love and truth without being judgmental. Their approach had a deep effect on their relationships. Instead of rejecting a pastor who had divorced his wife and left the ministry, they kept their door open and served as an instrument to help him recover his spiritual health. They didn't excuse his sin, yet they accepted him in a way that let him know he wasn't alone. Instead of making

Principle #4: As You Judge, You Will Be Judged

those who did not yet know Jesus feel like outsiders, they welcomed them as part of the family around the supper table and as fishing partners out on the lake. Instead of letting their concern that their daughter Chaundel was dating a very young Christian cause them to look down their spiritual noses, they welcomed me with open arms and became a major influence in my growth in loving Jesus and in my call to ministry.

If these words of Jesus are going to have any impact on our lives, we must reject the attractive yet cowardly and false interpretation of what he is saying. The cowardly approach to being nonjudgmental says, "You live your life, and I'll live mine. I won't say anything about your life, and you won't say anything about mine." Sounds good, doesn't it? We'd all like to avoid the unpleasantness of confronting problems in a relationship or in a friend's life. Even more, we don't like it when others confront the things we don't want to change in our own lives. It's interesting that right

> *Those who take to heart what Jesus teaches about judgment develop a more magnetic personality.*

after saying, "Do not judge," Jesus teaches, "Do not give dogs what is sacred; do not throw your pearls to pigs" (Matthew 7:6). He obviously has a different way of looking at things! He had no problem encouraging us to discern someone's willingness to listen to the truth. Not being judgmental doesn't mean you can't be discerning; nor does it mean you can't say it is right to do one thing and wrong to do another. If this were so, it would be ridiculous for Jesus to tell us to not judge—because that statement would itself be judgmental.

Being judgmental has to do with our judgment of people's

thoughts and motives. When we don't like someone, it's easy to attribute all their actions—even good ones—to bad motives. When we like someone, we tend to excuse their wrong actions by saying that they have a good heart. Both responses—falsely condemning and falsely excusing actions—are judgmental.

We live in a world that is confused about what judgment is and what it is not. We're all limited human beings who have a hard time judging our own motives, let alone those of others—which is exactly why we need the relational expertise of Jesus. In these verses from Matthew's gospel, Jesus teaches us three things about what it means to be nonjudgmental: (1) don't say one thing and do another—don't be a *hypocrite*; (2) judge yourself rightly and be willing to make changes— show that you have *integrity*; and (3) give to others the same kind of understanding, grace, and forgiveness that God has given you—make sure you show *mercy*.

Hypocrisy, integrity, and mercy—these are the words we'll focus on this week. Jesus used a simple picture of wood planks and sawdust specks in the eye to cut through all of our confusion. Hypocrisy is focusing on the speck in another person's eye while ignoring the two-by-four plank in your own. Integrity is removing the board from your own eye. Mercy is removing the speck from another's eye.

When I think of judgment, I'm drawn to the story of Jesus and the woman caught in adultery. She was dragged to see Jesus by a pack of hypocrites who pointed their fingers at her obvious sin but refused to look at their own obvious sins. Jesus stood in front of this crowd and challenged them to have the integrity to look for the sin in their own lives: "If any one of you is without sin, let him be the first to throw a stone at her" (John 8:7). Instead of throwing a stone, they all left, beginning with the oldest. Once everyone was gone, Jesus expressed redeeming mercy: "Neither do I condemn you.... Go now and leave your life of sin" (8:11).

I invite you to join me in this prayer:

Father, help me to understand this truth about judgment as never before. Instead of living in confusion about who and what I can rightly judge, help me to learn from you how to reject hypocrisy, choose integrity, and show mercy. Amen.

DAY TWENTY-TWO
Thinking about My Relationships

Point to Ponder: Hypocrisy is focusing on the speck in another person's eye while ignoring the plank in your own. Integrity is removing the plank from your own eye. Mercy is removing the speck from another's eye.

Verse to Remember: *"Do not judge, or you too will be judged"* (Matthew 7:1).

Question to Consider: Are there places in my life where I see a tendency to be judgmental of others?

Tomorrow: Say no to hypocrisy

23

Say No
to Hypocrisy

Hypocrisy is an easy target for humor. We remember stories
such as the one about the woman in the airport who sat down
to wait for a plane with a good book in hand and a bag of
chocolate chip cookies she'd bought at the airport store. She
hardly noticed when a man sat down two seats away from her
and began to read his newspaper. Seeing the bag of cookies
on the seat between them, she opened it up and took a cookie.
In the next moment, she couldn't help but notice the man,
because he reached his hand into the bag and helped himself
to a cookie. Not wanting to create a scene, the woman said
nothing. For the next few minutes she would eat a cookie,
then he'd eat a cookie. Her indignation increased with each
cookie he took. When only one cookie was left in the bag, he
took it out, broke it in two, and smiled as he gave her half. "Of
all the nerve," the woman thought. "It's amazing how some
people will act." Just then, the announcement came that the
flight was boarding. The man got up and headed toward the
plane. The woman grabbed her satchel, opened it to put her

book away, and saw *her* bag of cookies tucked away at the bottom of the satchel.

It's good to laugh at our hypocrisy. It's an admission of just how ridiculous it can be. In fact, when Jesus talked about hypocrisy, he did so with a touch of humor—which we may not recognize because we're not familiar with the humor by exaggeration of Jesus' day. These words of Jesus would have prompted a smile from those who first heard them: "How can you say to your brother, 'Let me take the speck out of your eye,' when all the time there is a plank in your own eye. You hypocrite!" (Matthew 7:4–5). Hypocrisy is looking at the speck in another person's eye and ignoring the board that is in your own eye.

> Take the road that leads to the freedom of a life without secrets, a life where you know that people love you for who you are, not for who you're pretending to be.

Jesus talked a lot about hypocrisy. In another conversation he said, "You are hypocrites! You wash the outside of your cups and dishes, but inside they are full of things you got by cheating others and by pleasing only yourselves" (Matthew 23:25 NCV). No humor this time—just a clear, to-the-heart challenge. Hypocrites are more concerned about appearance—washing the outside of the cup—than the reality of what's on the inside. And they love to put requirements on others that they're not willing to live up to themselves.

We easily think of hypocrisy as being something like holding an Alcoholics Anonymous meeting in a bar or a Weight Watchers' meeting at an ice cream shop. But Jesus expands the definition: Hypocrisy is pointing out the wrong in someone's life and being unwilling to consider or admit it in your own life. Hypocrisy is saying to our kids, "Do as I say and not as I do."

The word *hypocrisy* is derived from the Greek word for actors on the stage who spoke from behind masks held in front of their faces. Hypocrisy is all about hiding behind a mask. Why hide behind a mask? Because you think people will be more impressed with the mask than they are with you—and, most likely, because you are doing something behind the mask that you don't want other people to see.

It's easy and less threatening to wear masks, and so we all find ourselves doing it at times. Here's the question: "Do you want to be known for the mask or for the real you? Do you want to take a road that leads to having people think well of you but not really know you—the path of being trapped in a life of pretending to be what you are not?" This road leads to the place where you hear someone tell you they love you, and yet a voice inside you is saying, "You say you love me, but if you knew the truth about me, you wouldn't say that!" It's a wearying road to travel. Each night, your head hits the pillow exhausted from pretending to be something you're not.

You can take that road—or you can take a road that leads to the freedom of a life without secrets, a life where you know that people respect you and love you for who you are, not for who you're pretending to be.

How Will I Reject Hypocrisy?

The only way to put into practice these words of Jesus is one day at a time, one relationship at a time, one conversation at a time. Instead of judging people in your mind, choose to love them with your words and actions. "Don't just pretend that you love others. Really love them," wrote Paul (Romans 12:9 NLT). It's so easy to pretend. I'm shocked at how often I pretend to listen to the people I love most. My mind wanders off to something that seems so important, and I don't hear what is being said. Seeing my glassy-eyed stare, they ask, "Did you hear what I was saying?" This is the moment of truth. Do I continue to pretend, or will I come clean? Far too often I've said, "Sure, I heard you," and then tried to put together the pieces of the conversation in order to act as though I'd been listening all along. Why don't I just stop pretending? It would be so much more refreshing and real to say, "I'm so sorry; I wasn't listening. Please say that again."

Jesus once said to some people who were good at pretending, "Don't do your good deeds publicly, to be admired" (Matthew 6:1 NLT). Their life was all show and no substance. The truth is, people often feel trapped in hypocrisy. Your life becomes like one of those shows that plays on Broadway year after year. You wake up every morning—and the curtain goes up for another day, another show. You know you're pretending, but you just don't know how to play it any other way. This week, you can change that. This is one show that must *not* go on and on. You can close it down. You have the freedom to say, "It was all for show, and it's going to change."

Where do you find this freedom? It's found in asking yourself who you're living to impress. God declared to Samuel, "Man looks at the outward appearance, but the LORD looks at the heart" (1 Samuel 16:7). Live to impress people, and you'll end up focusing on the outward appearance— because that *is* what impresses people. You'll spend your life painting a better mask. Live your life to impress God, and it'll immediately be apparent that he sees right through the mask. God is not impressed with our pretending. There is tremendous freedom to be found in living your life for the sake of the one from whom you cannot hide, in whom you are most deeply loved, through whom you can live a life of significance, and with whom you will spend eternity.

DAY TWENTY-THREE
Thinking about My Relationships

Point to Ponder: Hypocrisy is being more concerned about appearance than reality.

Verse to Remember: *Don't just pretend that you love others. Really love them* (Romans 12:9 NLT).

Question to Consider: Is there some circumstance or relationship in my life where I've grown comfortable wearing a mask?

Tomorrow: Say yes to integrity

21

Say Yes
to Integrity

The second word in this picture Jesus gives us is *integrity*.
Hypocrisy is ignoring the plank in your eye. Integrity is
removing the plank from your eye. It's not enough just to
see the board in your eye; you must do something about it. I
have known people who will say, "I know I do a lot of rotten
things in my life, but I'm honest about what a selfish person I
am — so at least I'm not a hypocrite." It's similar to the person
afraid to run in a race who says, "Well, at least I didn't lose."
Of course you didn't. You never ran. You never took the risk!
Jesus said, "Start by getting the board out of your own eye."
Choose integrity.

You choose integrity when you see a fault in someone else
and immediately look at yourself to see if there are signs of
that same fault in you. You recognize that the wrong you see
in others may be an indication of a sin in your own life. Have
you noticed that it's easiest to notice the specks in others' eyes
when you have a plank of the same kind in your own eye? You
see in other people the very problems that are most common

in your own life. The person in the office whose personality most irritates you is probably more like you than you'd care to admit. Parents, I hate to tell you this, but the one child who most bugs you is typically the child who is most like you!

There is good news for your growth here: if you allow the faults of others to become a motivation for personal change, you'll never run out of motivation for change. And don't forget this: your faults can become the motivation for their growth and change. Think of the transforming impact in our lives if the faults of others became a motivation for growth instead of a motivation for gossip. Integrity is removing the plank from your eye.

> *Integrity means you make up your mind in advance to do the right thing.*

Getting the board out of your eye almost always means much more than noticing it and easily plucking it out. David wrote, "I know, my God, that you test the heart and are pleased with integrity" (1 Chronicles 29:17). Life is a test, and one of the main questions is your integrity. Everyone knows that to do well on a test you have to prepare in advance. Integrity means you make up your mind in advance to do the right thing. You don't wait until you get into a conversation to decide whether you'll tell the truth; you decide in advance. You don't wait until your sexual purity is tested to decide whether you'll be pure; you decide in advance.

One of the best ways to decide in advance is to tell someone else what you're planning to do. Years ago, a businessman in our church came to me to ask for advice about business practices in the accounting firm where he worked. He talked about his concern that, although some of these practices were legal, they were immoral. Instead of simply blaming others, he began by admitting the fault in his own life. His concerns had caused him to look at his own life and to ask questions about his own practices. He determined to make changes in his actions and to speak up about his concerns for the company. He didn't blame others. He took accountability for what he had done. He was willing to stand up and do the right thing—even if it meant losing his job. And he was willing to turn his desire for integrity into a decision to act with integrity by telling someone else what he was planning to do. Now that's a man of integrity!

How Will I Choose Integrity?

Whether it involves a small lie or a major deception, we all struggle with pretending. The question is this: "What are you going to do about it?" We could easily list hundreds of choices that reflect integrity in our daily lives. Here are just a few to get you started in choosing integrity:

Choose to Speak the Truth

Choose to speak the truth about yourself. On Day 18 we looked at the value of speaking the truth to *others*; Jesus' command to first get the plank out of our own eye (Matthew 7:5) tells us we'd better start with the truth about *ourselves*. The truth about yourself begins with a tough question: "Is there a lie have you been working overtime to keep covered?" I encourage you to do what may be the bravest thing you've ever done—ask God for the courage and strength to tell the truth.

Choose to Be Honest about Faults

James implores us, "Admit your faults to one another and pray for each other" (James 5:16 LB). What if I said, "Find the nearest person and do this right now"? "Whoa, be honest about my faults? My sins? That scares me to death. No way am I doing that!" James isn't telling us to admit our faults to *everyone*, but to admit them to *someone*— someone you can trust. How do you know you can trust someone? James 5:16 next says, "Pray for each other" — which isn't a bad place to start. Find someone who will pray for you. It's easy to find people who will excuse your faults, because your honesty about your sins makes them feel uncomfortable about their own. It's just as easy to find others who will tell you how bad your fault really is, because it makes them feel better about their own. But if you can find just one person who will truly listen to you, who will take you seriously and pray for you, you have found a good friend. If you have just one person like this in your life, you are a truly blessed person. If you have more than one, you are blessed beyond measure!

Choose to Ask for God's Help

King David speaks passionately about the choice for integrity and the need for God's help:

> I will try to walk a blameless path, but how I need your help, especially in my own home, where I long to act as I should.
>
> Help me to refuse the low and vulgar things; help me to abhor all crooked deals of every kind, to have no part in them.
>
> Psalm 101:2-3 LB

Integrity is about determining to walk the right path. Integrity is about asking for God's help. Integrity is about saying no—about refusing to pursue low and vulgar things. Integrity is about what happens in my own home, where no one else sees but my own heart certainly knows.

When we think of low and vulgar things, we immediately think of pornography on the Internet or on cable TV, which is having a devastating impact on Christian families. Integrity means saying no to pornography. Other low and vulgar things make their way into our homes as well. Speaking cruel and profane words, letting our anger burn out of control, and gossiping around the table are low and vulgar things. God made us to look to him for so much more than this. The psalmist tells us, "The LORD on high is mighty" (Psalm 93:4). Integrity is choosing to ask for God's help to say no. Integrity is recognizing that without God's help we don't have the power to say no, but that with his help we have a new power to say yes to high and mighty things.

Thinking about My Relationships

Point to Ponder: Integrity means making up your mind in advance to do the right thing.

Verse to Remember: *I know, my God, that you test the heart and are pleased with integrity* (1 Chronicles 29:17).

Question to Consider: Who in your life can you admit your faults to and be confident that they will pray for you?

Tomorrow: Say now to mercy

25

Say Now to Mercy

We've seen that hypocrisy is focusing on the speck in another's eye while ignoring the plank in your own, and integrity is removing the plank from your own eye. Today we reflect on this truth: mercy is removing the speck from your brother's or sister's eye. Once you've taken the board out of your own eye, then Jesus tells you to have the mercy to remove the speck out of someone else's eye.

Jesus didn't tell you to pretend there's not a speck in your friend's eye or to only be concerned about the plank in your eye. He urged you to get the plank out of your eye—and then you can see clearly enough to help your friend get the speck out of his or her eye. How are you going to help your friend if you can't say, "I noticed there's a speck in your eye. Can I help?"

We live in a society that believes the opposite of judgment is tolerance. And tolerance is falsely defined as accepting without opinion or comment whatever choices another makes. But Jesus told us the alternative to judgment is not tolerance; it is mercy. The alternative to being judgmental is not ignoring other people's faults; it is showing that Jesus has forgiven all our faults.

Being biblically nonjudgmental does not mean we pretend we don't see another person's sin. To do so would be living in denial. Of course we see each other's sins—many of them are *very* obvious. The question is this: "What will we do about it?" Being nonjudgmental means we recognize that we all face the same temptations. It means we don't see anyone as outside the circle of God's grace, as beyond the bounds of our forgiveness, as outside the limits of our love.

> No one is outside the circle of God's grace, beyond the bounds of our forgiveness, outside the limits of our love.

Jesus is teaching an advanced degree course in relationships. This isn't easy. I certainly struggle with learning how to show mercy without judgment. It's easy to be judgmental and end up gossiping about someone's problem rather than offering care.

It's just as easy to settle for a false "mercy" that offers care but lacks the courage to tell the truth.

As I read the words of Jesus, the most shocking and controversial thing he teaches us about our mercy toward others is this: *mercy is not optional*—not if you want to experience and enjoy the mercy of God yourself.

"Wait just a minute," the theologically astute will say. "Doesn't God say that his mercy is a free gift based on his grace, not on anything I can do? How can you say I must show mercy to others in order to enjoy his mercy?" They are right, of course. Salvation is *not* a work that we do; it certainly *is* a gift of God. This is a truth I believe in the depth of my soul. Yet this belief sometimes leads us to a strange place when it comes to the way we receive and give mercy. We believe God has shown his mercy to us, and we've accepted this gift through faith. His mercy and forgiveness are guaranteed by his very love. But when it comes to our expressions of mercy toward others, we seem to think they are subject to our all too human frailties. Sometimes we forgive; sometimes we say we just can't. We choose to show mercy to some but decide that others aren't deserving of our mercy because of the depth of hurt they've caused. Jesus put his finger on this kind of thinking and called it clearly wrong.

At the end of the Lord's Prayer, after teaching his disciples to pray, "Forgive us our sins, just as we have forgiven those who have sinned against us" (Matthew 6:12 NLT), Jesus said this: "If you forgive those who sin against you, your heavenly Father will forgive you. But if you refuse to forgive others, your Father will not forgive your sins" (6:14–15 NLT).

Later in Matthew's gospel, Jesus told a story about a man who had been forgiven an enormous debt, yet refused to forgive a small debt owed to him:

> "When that servant went out, he found one of his fellow servants who owed him a hundred denarii. He grabbed him and began to choke him. 'Pay back what you owe me!' he demanded.
>
> "His fellow servant fell to his knees and begged him, 'Be patient with me, and I will pay you back.'
>
> "But he refused. Instead, he went off and had the man thrown into prison until he could pay the debt. When the other servants saw what had happened, they were greatly distressed and went and told their master everything that had happened.

"Then the master called the servant in. 'You wicked servant,' he said, 'I canceled all that debt of yours because you begged me to. Shouldn't you have had mercy on your fellow servant just as I had on you?' In anger his master turned him over to the jailers to be tortured, until he should pay back all he owed.

"This is how my heavenly Father will treat each of you unless you forgive your brother from your heart."

Matthew 18:28-35

If our forgiveness from God is not based on any work we can do, how could Jesus say such things? Because he knows the human heart. Jesus knows that those who cannot find it in them to forgive haven't truly understood what it means to be forgiven. The debtor in Jesus' story heard words of forgiveness, but his actions toward his fellow servant showed that the words never reached his heart.

If you're struggling somewhere in your life with an inability to forgive, you may be thinking, "You're not being very merciful toward *me* right now. You haven't been through what I've been through. Showing mercy—forgiving that person—is just so difficult." The more deeply you've been hurt, the more your mind rebels against the thought of forgiveness. Jesus helps you with this struggle by not pulling any punches. The words I've shared with you are not mine; they are the words of Jesus. Why would Jesus be so seemingly harsh and insensitive on this issue—especially when it touches such a deep place of hurt in your life? Yes, he knows your hurt. He knows how difficult it is to forgive. He died on a cross to pay the price for our sins; yes, he knows forgiveness isn't easy! Jesus also knows that a flat-out refusal to forgive is a sure indication of what is going on in a person's heart. He knows how easily we can allow bitterness to first stain and then destroy all of our relationships.

He knows how Satan loves to use our refusal to forgive someone to keep us from the transforming forgiveness of God.

> Mercy is the proper response of those who have received God's mercy.

Let me be clear here. I'm not talking about the time it can take to process through our emotions and faith and choose to forgive; I'm talking about going year after year with a lack of mercy in your mind toward someone. Nor am I talking about trust, but about forgiveness. If someone steals money from your company, if you ever trust them again with your finances it will only be after that trust has been regained over time. Trust will take time to rebuild—and it may never be rebuilt. Yet merciful forgiveness is to be offered immediately. Mercy is the proper response of those who have received God's mercy.

How Will I Show Mercy?

Of the three—rejecting hypocrisy, choosing integrity, and showing mercy—genuine mercy takes the most courage. Why? Because mercy is often rejected. People reject God's mercy all the time—and his mercy is perfect. So naturally they'll reject our imperfect expressions of mercy.

Mercy is always to be offered, but it is not always accepted. If you think people will always respond well to your acts of mercy, you're kidding yourself. When I'm angry at someone who responds with kindness toward me, it can make me even angrier. I stubbornly want to stay angry, and I'm not happy that someone is putting a finger on a sensitive, prideful nerve. When you say to someone, "Can I help you get that speck out of your eye?" you'll get all kinds of reactions: "What speck?" "Who do you think you are?" "Keep your nose out of my business." "Keep your finger out of my eye!" What do you do when your offer of mercy is rejected? Do what Jesus did: continue to show mercy. He offered merciful forgiveness even while being ridiculed, rejected, and nailed to a cross.

When you're offering mercy, remember that we often initially see mercy as a threat rather than an expression of love. We treat God this way all of the time. Instead of feeling drawn in by the love and forgiveness of Jesus, we feel threatened by how God could step in and "mess up my life." When you are rejected for an expression of kind mercy, remember that you are in very good company.

Courageous mercy can be shown in practical ways every day. Paul gives wonderful insight into how to express mercy:

> God has chosen you and made you his holy people. He loves you. So always do these things: Show mercy to others, be kind, humble, gentle, and patient. Get along with each other, and forgive each other. If someone does wrong to you, forgive that person because the Lord forgave you.
>
> Colossians 3:12–13 NCV

Everything in these verses points to how we can show mercy to people around us. Look for places today where you can make the choices you see listed in this verse:

• *Be kind.* Kind words and actions are simple expressions

of mercy that make more of a difference than you'll ever realize. Whether to a family member or to the cashier at the grocery store, a kind word has the power to rearrange someone's day.

- *Be humble.* When you make the choice to speak with humility about yourself or to act in humility toward others, you are expressing in some small measure the mercy Jesus showed us when he humbled himself to come to this earth to serve us. Humility is a risk. But unless someone chooses to act in humility in your family or at school or the office, relationships will be blocked by the logjam of pride.

- *Be gentle*—especially with your words. *Gentle* does not necessarily mean *quiet*. It means *unselfish*—admitting where you are wrong. You stop assigning blame and start accepting responsibility. There is amazing power in your choice to use a gentle tone and gentle words: "A gentle answer will calm a person's anger, but an unkind answer will cause more anger" (Proverbs 15:1 NCV).

- *Be patient.* When you're patient with someone, you are mercifully recognizing you need others' patience as well.

- *Get along with people.* "Oh no, not that too," you say. "Don't tell me I actually have to work to get along with people!" You won't agree with everyone you meet today, but you can try to get along with everyone you meet. Paul writes elsewhere, "If it is possible, as far as it depends on you, live at peace with everyone" (Romans 12:18).

- *Forgive.* Colossians 3:12–13 ends with the greatest expression of mercy one person can show another, namely, forgiveness. If you're struggling to forgive someone, ask God for the strength to do what you cannot do on your own. Paul points to the power that can equip you for forgiving: "Forgive that person because the Lord forgave you" (NCV). The strength to forgive someone else can only be found in the truth that you have been forgiven by God.

The Old Testament prophet Micah wrote these familiar words: "And what does the LORD require of you? To act justly and to love mercy and to walk humbly with your God" (Micah 6:8). Concerning the love for mercy, Gary Thomas writes, "We've all heard of believers who rail against someone else's sin — only to discover later that they were enmeshed in exactly that struggle. When we fail to fall in love with mercy, we often deal with our own sin by denouncing it in others. In contrast, mercy invites us to admit our guilt, receive God's forgiveness, and then stop judging others."[*]

William Shakespeare's famous quote is a picture of the beauty and the blessing of mercy:

> *The quality of mercy is not strain'd,*
> *It droppeth as the gentle rain from heaven*
> *Upon the place beneath. It is twice bless'd:*
> *It blesseth him that gives and him that takes.*[†]

The last word goes to Jesus: "Blessed are the merciful, for they will be shown mercy" (Matthew 5:7).

---

[*] Gary Thomas, "Blessed Are the Merciful," *Discipleship Journal* 138 (November/December 2003): 60.
[†] William Shakespeare, "The Merchant of Venice," Act IV, section 1.

Thinking about My Relationships

Point to Ponder: The alternative to judgment is not tolerance; it is mercy.

Verses to Remember: *God has chosen you and made you his holy people. He loves you. So always do these things: Show mercy to others, be kind, humble, gentle, and patient. Get along with each other, and forgive each other. If someone does wrong to you, forgive that person because the Lord forgave you* (Colossians 3:12–13 NCV).

Question to Consider: To whom can I show mercy today?

Tomorrow: Understanding God's mercy

26

Understanding
God's Mercy

EXPERIENCE THE TRUTH

You've just arrived for a wonderful meal in the beautiful home of one of the most influential men in Israel—Simon the Pharisee. Before the meal begins, an uninvited guest slips in to see Jesus. Although uninvited, she is not unknown to those at the meal. This woman is notorious for her immorality; she is a prostitute. And she wants to see Jesus. How uncomfortable! Oh, maybe Jesus *should* talk with her, but this just isn't the right time or place.

And then the uncomfortable gets embarrassing! She begins to weep as she stands behind Jesus, first softly and then quite noticeably. Everyone at the party acts as if they don't see the obvious. This woman then does something no one can ignore—she bows before Jesus and lets her tears begin to splash gently onto his dirty feet. You can almost sense the room going quiet—no one knows what to do or say.

Then the unthinkable happens. This woman takes her hair—her hair!—and begins to wipe her tears from Jesus' feet. In that culture, prostitutes let their hair go unbound in public; proper women kept their hair covered. This woman obviously didn't know how to act in polite company. She seemed to be flaunting her immorality!

She then pours perfume on Jesus' feet and finishes wiping them with her hair. As the fragrance fills the room, you can imagine the thoughts that filled people's minds: "This is ridiculous. Doesn't Jesus know how bad this looks? What a waste to pour perfume on dirty feet. This woman doesn't belong here!"

We don't have to imagine what Simon thought. The Bible tells us Jesus' host said to himself, "If Jesus were a prophet, he would know who this woman was and wouldn't let her touch him."

Jesus knew Simon's thoughts and had an answer for him. Before listening in on his answer, ask yourself a question: "What would I have thought?" It's easy to look down our self-righteous noses at Simon in hindsight. If you had been there that day, wouldn't you have felt at least a little embarrassed?

Jesus wasn't embarrassed in the least. He saw past the social niceties and cultural difficulties into this woman's heart. And he tells a simple story to help us see her heart also—a story about two people who were forgiven a debt: "Two men owed money to a certain moneylender. One owed him five hundred denarii, and the other fifty. Neither of them had the money to pay him back, so he canceled the debts of both. Now which of them will love him more?" The answer is obvious: the one who was forgiven the greatest debt.

Jesus then paints a picture for Simon that teaches profound truth about love. He says to Simon, "You did not even wash my feet with water, but this woman washed my feet with her tears. You didn't even give me oil for my head [a common kindness for a guest with hair that was dirty from the dust of traveling], but she poured perfume on my feet." Jesus showed Simon the heart of a woman who loved Jesus deeply because she knew how much she had been forgiven. Jesus concludes with this amazing principle of love: The one who is forgiven much loves much; the one who is forgiven little loves little.

Based on Luke 7:36-50

Wow! When you boil it all down, you've got one of two choices: you can be like Simon—grateful you've lived a more moral life than most other people; or you can be like the woman—grateful for *how much* you have been forgiven. Jesus teaches that those who make the choice this woman made—even to the point of embarrassment—deepen their love for him.

God wants us to be merciful because *he* is merciful. God's

mercy is overwhelming! The secret to a heart of mercy is in seeing—really seeing—God's mercy toward you. The better you understand the mercy God has given to you, the more merciful you'll be toward others.

The grace and mercy of God are his undeserved gifts to us. If you could earn God's favor, you could easily become judgmental toward those who had not earned what you had. The Bible directs *all of us* to come boldly to God's throne, "so that we may receive mercy and find grace to help us in our time of need" (Hebrews 4:16).

> *The better you understand the mercy God has given to you, the more merciful you'll be toward others.*

I'll never forget the picture of grace and mercy I received as a junior high boy. Mr. and Mrs. Powell were a kind older couple who lived next door. Mrs. Powell had over twenty canaries and a large tank of tropical fish we took care of when they were away. When I was in junior high, she decided, "Tommy's old enough. I'll pay him to take care of the birds and the fish while we're away for a week." I took the job. All I needed to do was feed the canaries and the tropical fish once a day. I could do that. It went well until about the third day, when a cold snap came through town. It was colder than it had been for years. I went over to feed the birds that morning. As I opened the door to the back shed that enclosed the atrium, something didn't look quite right. I went back and asked my mom, "Mom, when birds sleep, do they lay on the ground with their feet sticking up in the air?" All twenty-one of the canaries had died—*all* of them. If only that were the end of the story. Two days later, the pump in the fish tank stopped working, and when I went to feed them in the morning, I found that all the fish had died as well.

Needless to say, I wasn't looking forward to the Powells' return home! When they got back, with downcast eyes I nervously stammered out the story of what had happened. Mrs. Powell showed me kindness. Instead of pointing out what I might have done differently, she said, "It wasn't your fault. It's going to be OK."

But then, as I was quickly heading out the door, she did something else. She stopped me, handed me an envelope, and said, "Here is your money for taking care of my fish and birds." I said, "I can't take that." She said, "No, you *have* to take it." Now that was an undeserved gift!

It wasn't until years later that I realized she must have read *Les Misérables*. Remember Victor Hugo's story of Jean Valjean—a common beggar and thief shown kindness by a bishop who takes him into his home? Valjean repays the bishop's kindness by stealing the silver spoons and forks from the home and fleeing into the night. By chance, he is stopped by policemen, who discover he has the silver and take him back to the bishop's house. The bishop could have easily said, "Yes, he took them." Valjean would have been condemned to spend the rest of his life in prison. Instead, in an incredible act of grace, the bishop said, "Yes, I wanted you to have those. In fact, you forgot these two silver candlesticks"—and he gave him the candlesticks as well.

Later in the book, Hugo writes of those two silver candlesticks: "All of Jean Valjean is contained in them."[*] All of his life, all of his identity, was contained in that one act of grace.

---

*Victor Hugo, *Les Misérables* (New York: Penguin, 1987), 233.

That is the intent of God's mercy, of God's grace. All of our lives are meant to be contained in his act of grace—what God has given us in and through Jesus Christ. Your forgiveness is contained in that act of grace. Your future is contained in that act of grace. Your relationships with God and with others are contained in God's great act of grace.

DAY TWENTY-SIX
Thinking about My Relationships

Point to Ponder: God wants us to be merciful because *he* is merciful.

Verses to Remember: *It is by grace you have been saved, through faith—and this not from yourselves, it is the gift of God—not by works, so that no one can boast* (Ephesians 2:8–9).

Question to Consider: Have I accepted God's gift of merciful forgiveness and the grace to live a new life?

Tomorrow: Understanding God's judgment

Understanding
God's Judgment

The skill of responding to another person's actions with integrity and mercy but not with hypocrisy is one of the most difficult relationship skills any of us can develop. Some veer too far on the side of excusing sins, others on the side of prideful judgment—few of us ever get it totally right. One of the keys to strengthening this skill is growing in our understanding of God's judgment over all mankind.

Words about judgment are difficult for many of us. We know God is a God of love, grace, and beauty. Something in us cringes when we see such words as *judge* and *judgment* attached to the name of God. So we naturally drift toward ignoring these words and focusing on the words that feel warmer and more loving. There are just too many uncomfortable questions that flood our minds when we think about judgment.

When you try to figure out all of the ways of the judgments of God, of course you're going to feel uncomfortable and confused. This is because God is the judge, and you are

not. I don't intend this to sound flippant or simplistic—
because it is not. The answer to figuring out the judgments
of God isn't found in philosophical understanding; it is found
in personal trust. God, who loves this world and everyone
in it more than I could ever hope to, is the ultimate judge. I
can trust him. God, who sees every injustice that has ever
been done and knows every motive of every heart, is the final
judge. I can trust him.

The truth about God's judgment could fill volumes. Here
our focus is on how an understanding of God's judgment
will cause us to be less judgmental. It is all too easy to
think that those who recognize God as judge become more
judgmental—but the opposite is true. Understanding God's
judgment frees you to not have to be judgmental, because
you know God is the judge. Freedom from being judgmental
comes as you remember the truths that God will judge fairly,
that now is not yet the time for final judgment, and that you
can face that day with confidence because you know and trust
God, who is rich in mercy and forgiveness.

The More I Trust God as the Only Fair Judge, the Less Judgmental I'll Be

To have healthy relationships there is a decision you must
make: leave judgment—ultimate judgment—in God's hands.
Practice what Paul tells us: "Do not take revenge, my friends,
but leave room for God's wrath, for it is written, 'It is mine to
avenge; I will repay,' says the Lord" (Romans 12:19). Let God
work out his judgment. Trust in the truth that God will judge
fairly.

It's not always easy to trust this truth—especially when

you've been hurt. As a young believer, I was profoundly affected by the story of Corrie ten Boom. She and her family had suffered in a Nazi concentration camp during World War II because they had hidden Jewish families in their home. The gripping story of her faith experiences in that camp are recounted in the book and movie *The Hiding Place*. It was years after her release from the camp, however, that her belief in God's justice, judgment, and forgiveness was most powerfully tested:

> It was in a church in Munich that I saw him — a balding, heavyset man in a gray overcoat, a brown felt hat clutched between his hands. People were filing out of the basement room where I had just spoken.... It was 1947 and I had come from Holland to defeated Germany with the message that God forgives....
>
> And that's when I saw him, working his way forward against the others. One moment I saw the overcoat and the brown hat; the next, a blue uniform and a visored cap with its skull and crossbones. It came back with a rush: the huge room [at the concentration camp called Ravensbruck] with its harsh overhead lights; the pathetic pile of dresses and shoes in the center of the floor; the shame of walking naked past this man.... The man who was making his way forward had been a guard — one of the most cruel guards.
>
> Now he was in front of me, hand thrust out: "A fine message, Fraulein! How good it is to know that, as you say, all our sins are at the bottom of the sea!"
>
> And I, who had spoken so glibly of forgiveness, fumbled in my pocketbook rather than take that hand. He would not remember me, of course — how could

he remember one prisoner among those thousands of women? But I remembered him and the leather crop swinging from his belt. I was face-to-face with one of my captors and my blood seemed to freeze.

"You mentioned Ravensbruck in your talk," he was saying. "I was a guard there." No, he did not remember me. "But since that time," he went on, "I have become a Christian. I know that God has forgiven me for the cruel things I did there, but I would like to hear it from your lips as well. Fraulein," — again the hand came out — "will you forgive me?"

And I stood there — I whose sins had again and again to be forgiven — and could not forgive. [My sister] Betsie had died in that place — could he erase her slow terrible death simply for the asking?

It could not have been many seconds that he stood there — hand held out — but to me it seemed hours as I wrestled with the most difficult thing I had ever had to do.

For I had to do it — I knew that.... I knew it not only as a commandment of God, but as a daily experience. Since the end of the war I had had a home in Holland for victims of Nazi brutality. Those who were able to forgive their former enemies were able also to return to the outside world and rebuild their lives, no matter what the physical scars. Those who nursed their bitterness remained invalids. It was as simple and as horrible as that.

And still I stood there with the coldness clutching my heart. But forgiveness is not an emotion — I knew that too. Forgiveness is an act of the will, and the will can function regardless of the temperature of the heart. "Jesus, help me!" I prayed silently. "I can lift my hand. I can do that much. You supply the feeling."

And so woodenly, mechanically, I thrust my hand into the one stretched out to me. And as I did, an incredible thing took place. The current started in my shoulder, raced down my arm, sprang into our joined hands. And then this healing warmth seemed to flood my whole being, bringing tears to my eyes.

"I forgive you, brother!" I cried. "With all my heart."

For a long moment we grasped each other's hands, the former guard and the former prisoner. I had never known God's love so intensely as I did then.[*]

One of the reasons we struggle to forgive is because deep down we're not always sure God is going to do a good enough job of judging those who have hurt us. Maybe he won't take note of how terrible their sin really was. Maybe they'll get saved and forgiven before they get punished. So we decide to take care of it ourselves. They hurt us, and we want the satisfaction of seeing them judged. We become less judgmental when we trust God as the only fair judge. The Bible tells us that God is able to judge our inmost thoughts and motives (Romans 2:16). I often cannot see the inner motives in my own life, so I certainly can't judge anyone else's inmost thoughts and motives. But God can! We can commit judgment into his hands.

The More I Trust God's Timing, the Less Judgmental I'll Be

The truth that God will judge in his time keeps me from yielding to the temptation to rush to judgment. Paul writes,

---

[*]Corrie ten Boom, *Tramp for the Lord* (Old Tappan, N.J.: Revell, 1974), 55–57.

"Judge nothing before the appointed time; wait till the Lord comes. He will bring to light what is hidden in darkness and will expose the motives of men's hearts. At that time each will receive his praise from God" (1 Corinthians 4:5). Jesus said, "All who reject me and my message will be judged at the Day of Judgment by the truths I have spoken" (John 12:48 LB). Healthy relationships demand I await ultimate judgment until his time. Sometimes we act as though we are two questions into a thousand-question test and already we want to give the grade. We may be able to see something of how we and others are doing so far, but we cannot give the final score.

> Healthy relation-ships demand we await ultimate judgment until God's time.

Jesus once told a story about wheat and weeds growing together in a field. The servants of the owner wondered if they should go and pull up the weeds. The owner responded, "No,... because while you are pulling the weeds, you may root up the wheat with them. Let both grow together until the harvest. At that time I will tell the harvesters: First collect the weeds and tie them in bundles to be burned; then gather the wheat and bring it into my barn'" (Matthew 13:29–30).

When we try to separate the wheat from the weeds, inevitably we'll make mistakes and do damage. Leave judgment until God's time. You can trust God to give praise to whom it is due; you can trust God to give justice to whom it is due. British essayist Thomas Carlyle once said, "Foolish men imagine that because judgment for an evil thing is delayed, there is no justice, but an accidental one, here below. Judgment for an evil thing is many times delayed some day or two, some century or two, but it is sure as life, it is sure as death!"*

The More Confidently I Face the Day of Judgment, the Less Judgmental I'll Be

Some people get nervous reading Jesus' words in Matthew 16:27 (NLT): "For I, the Son of Man, will come in the glory of my Father with his angels and will judge all people according to their deeds." Judge *all people*—that includes me! If this makes you anxious, then Romans 2:16 (LB) will make you break out in a sweat: "The day will surely come when at God's command Jesus Christ will judge the secret lives of everyone, their inmost thoughts and motives; this is all part of God's great plan which I proclaim." Judge my secret life! That doesn't sound like a "great plan" to most of us.

Put alongside these verses these words from 1 John 4:17 (LB): "As we live with Christ, our love grows more perfect and complete; so we will not be ashamed and embarrassed at the day of judgment, but can face him with confidence and joy, because he loves us and we love him too." Face him with confidence! Not be ashamed or embarrassed! How is that going to happen? The idea of facing God with confidence on judgment day is foreign to many of us. A popular picture of judgment places me in a line that snakes its way toward a huge desk at the entrance to heaven. Saint Peter is sitting in an enormous chair at a gigantic desk with an imposing book in front of him that will tell me whether I'm "in" or "out." As I stand in line, I say to myself, "I think I've trusted Christ. I've

---

*Thomas Carlyle, *Chartism: Past and Present* (Chestnut Hill, Mass.: Adamant Media, 2001), 76.

done my best to trust Christ." But each time I move up a step, my anxiety doubles. "Did I really trust him as I should have?" Finally I get to the front of the line. "Did I get in?!?" Peter looks slowly through the Book of Life, turning the pages with painful precision, until he sees my name. "I'm in! Hooray!"

This is a totally false picture. John's gospel tells us that if you know Jesus, you've already passed from judgment to life: "In all truth I tell you, whoever listens to my words, and believes in the one who sent me, has eternal life; without being brought to judgment such a person has passed from death to life" (John 5:24 NJB). It's already settled; you're not even waiting anxiously in that long line if you have listened to and trusted Jesus. You don't have to worry about heaven and hell judgment any longer because you know him. You know one day you'll face him with confidence and joy because he loves you and you love him. You—and anyone who has accepted the gift of God's mercy and forgiveness—can live with that confidence.

According to a 2003 Pew Research Poll, eight in ten Americans agree we will all be called before God to answer for our sins.* And we know that God is the ultimate judge, not us. That leaves some living with a worry in the back of their mind: "Someday I'll have to face God, and he'll get me for all of the things I've done." If you feel this way about God, you probably don't have a great desire to be close to him; we tend to avoid people we think are out to get us. God is *not* out to get you. He has set his heart to love you and has invited you

---

*Pew Research Center, "Religion in American Life," in *The 2004 Political Landscape*, released November 5, 2003, *http://people-press.org/reports/display.php3?PageID=757.*

Principle #4: As You Judge, You Will Be Judged

into a confident relationship with him that will last for all eternity.

The fact of God's judgment should affect every moment of my life. Peter writes, "Remember that your heavenly Father to whom you pray has no favorites when he judges. He will judge you with perfect justice for everything you do; so act in reverent fear of him from now on until you get to heaven" (1 Peter 1:17 LB). The reality that someday I'm going to be judged by God should cause me to act in reverent fear of him. What does "reverent fear" mean? It means I won't be afraid of that day, but instead I will respect God's person and power as I live for that day.

DAY TWENTY-SEVEN
Thinking about My Relationships

Point to Ponder: The more I trust God as judge, the less judgmental I'll be.

Verse to Remember: *Judge nothing before the appointed time; wait till the Lord comes. He will bring to light what is hidden in darkness and will expose the motives of men's hearts. At that time each will receive his praise from God* (1 Corinthians 4:5).

Question to Consider: Am I trusting God to judge fairly?

Tomorrow: Seeing the truth about yourself

Seeing the Truth
about Yourself

Of late I've been making trips to the eye doctor. For the past
few years I've been noticing they must be making the print
on CD covers smaller and smaller. I went to the eye doctor,
and he told me the problem wasn't with the print but with my
eyes. I had "presbyopia"—which has nothing to do with being
Presbyterian. There is a time when it's a bad thing to know
a little Greek. In Greek *presbys* means "elder," and *opia* means
"eyes." This word is just a nice way of telling me I have old
eyes!

Each time I go to the ophthalmologist I take the standard
"eye test." I look at the wall and read the lines of letters as far
down the chart as I can.

ZOECFLDPBT

ETOLEBZEF

BOFCPTEBL

I'd like to do a different kind of test with you right

now—not an "eye test," but an "I test." The more clearly you can read the two lines below, the more clearly you'll be able to apply Jesus' principle of judgment and mercy in your life.

I HAVE SINNED
I AM FORGIVEN

The better you *see* these two truths, the less judgmental and the more merciful you will become.

Paul tells the terrible truth when he writes, "No one is good—not even one. No one has real understanding; no one is seeking God. All have turned away from God; all have gone wrong.... For all have sinned; all fall short of God's glorious standard" (Romans 3:10–12, 23 NLT). I have sinned; you have sinned. When we pretend that we haven't, we have problems with judgment. People who act as though they've never sinned are the most judgmental people on earth. Those who think the only sins they've committed are "little sins" are the most condemning people you'll ever meet. As believers in Jesus, we should be the least judgmental of all because we know how much we have been forgiven.

Paul tells the wonderful truth when he writes, "We are made right in God's sight when we trust in Jesus Christ to take away our sins. And we all can be saved in this same way, no matter who we are or what we have done.... Yet now God in his gracious kindness declares us not guilty. He has done this through Christ Jesus, who has freed us by taking away our sins" (Romans 3:22, 24 NLT). I am forgiven; you are forgiven! We are gloriously declared not guilty through our trust in Jesus Christ.

When I see that I have sinned and have been forgiven, I

am empowered to become a less judgmental person. The more clearly I see both of these truths, the less judgmental I'll be. And I do need to see both. If all I see is that I've sinned, I still feel my guilt and become even more judgmental. If all I see is that I've been forgiven, forgetting the fact that I'm a sinner who needs forgiveness for daily sins, I will struggle with being judgmental. Why is it that some who have been Christians for years become more and more judgmental? Because they have forgotten how deeply they need God's grace. When God's Word helps me see both truths clearly — I have sinned, and I am forgiven — it gives me the power to live out the "no condemnation/forgiving/giving to others no matter what their need or struggle" lifestyle Jesus modeled. "Mercy triumphs over judgment!" (James 2:13).

When we think of how Jesus loved without condemning, many would say the most powerful example is his treatment of the woman caught in adultery. To me, an even more powerful picture of his nonjudgmental love is found in his treatment of a disciple caught in doubt. The woman, you see, didn't know Jesus — she hadn't yet discovered the power he had to change her life. It's much easier to keep from condemning when someone

> We should be the least judgmental of all because we know how much we have been forgiven.

has never heard the truth. The most difficult person to not judge is the person who "should have known better." It's often easier to offer nonjudgmental love to a stranger who has sinned horribly than to a friend who has disappointed you. We can learn from the way Jesus loved his friend Thomas:

Thomas should have known better. He had followed Jesus as one of his disciples for three years. He'd experienced every miracle, heard every teaching, and seen every example. When Jesus declared himself to be "the resurrection and the life," Thomas was there. When Jesus then proceeded to raise Lazarus from the dead (John 11:25, 43), Thomas was there. When Jesus told his followers, "After three days I'll rise again" (Mark 8:31), Thomas was there.

But when the resurrected Jesus first appeared to his gathered disciples in an upper room, Thomas was not there. It may have been for a valid reason. (Maybe he went out to get Starbucks for the rest of the disciples!) Whatever the case, he was not in the room. So he missed the electric thrill of faith that occurred when Jesus appeared to the disciples—alive! The room was still buzzing when Thomas returned. The other disciples must have fallen over themselves to be the first to tell him the news: "Jesus is alive! We just saw him."

Thomas's response? "I don't believe it. I won't believe it! I have to not only see Jesus myself but also touch him before I'll believe it!"

Thomas should have known better. When Jesus appeared to him and the other disciples a week later, it would have been easy to condemn: "Thomas, I expected better things from you after following me for three years." "Thomas, how could you not trust the word of ten other disciples?" "Thomas, why do you want to wallow in your doubt?"

Jesus said none of those things. Instead, he offered his friend nonjudgmental love. "Thomas, you said you needed to touch my hands and my side. Go ahead." Doubting Thomas immediately became Trusting Thomas. "My Lord and my God!" he exclaimed in one of the greatest declarations of faith ever expressed.

Based on John 20:24 - 29

A Self-Test

The following list of questions will help you test yourself in this area of judgment with the goal that you will develop better relationships. These questions won't be easy on you; they will spur you toward growth and change. If you are willing first to ask them and then to listen for God's answers, three things will happen:

- *You will be changed*; integrity will replace hypocrisy in hidden areas of your life.
- *Your relationships will be changed*; they'll breathe in the fresh air of mercy.
- *Those around you will be changed*; they will experience the loving, merciful touch of someone who knows how to remove a speck from a brother's or sister's eye.

Jesus chose the perfect picture when he talked about taking a speck out of someone's eye. The eye is a very sensitive area. If someone is going to help get something out of my eye, it needs to be someone I trust. I'm not letting just anyone mess with my eye! The way we earn this kind of trust is to show the people we love we're working on our own lives as well.

Take a moment to read through these questions. Then find a time when you won't be interrupted for at least thirty minutes, and go over them again. You may want to schedule several hours to be away in the mountains, beside a lake or stream, or at the beach. Just you and God having a talk about eyes and planks and specks, about hypocrisy and integrity and mercy.

Questions about Ignoring the Plank in My Eye

What do I know to be true that I'm pretending is not true ...

> in my relationships with others?
> in my relationship with God?
> in my thought life?
> in my business life?
> in my finances?
> in my recreation?

Do I find myself filled with anxiety or anger? What may be causing these emotions?

Is there something I know God has told me to do that I still haven't done?

Have I been focusing on the sins of others in order to hide from my own sin?

Questions about Removing the Plank from My Eye

Have I confessed my sin to God?

Have I confessed my sin to another person and sought forgiveness?

Do I have an accountability partner with whom I meet regularly for my spiritual health?

If I struggle with an addiction, what is keeping me from getting involved in a recovery program?

Have I made restitution if needed in cases where I've cheated or hurt someone?

Is there someone I need to forgive?

Questions about Removing the Speck from My Brother's or Sister's Eye

Have I first looked for this issue or problem in my own life?

When will I talk with this person I want to help?

How should I pray specifically before we talk?

How can I state things in such a way that a spirit of mercy comes through?

What will I do if he or she responds well to our conversation? (Determine in advance what advice and support you can give!)

What will you do if he or she does not respond well to your conversation? (Determine in advance to choose to love, even if you are put off or rejected.)

As these days of considering the principle "As you judge, you will be judged" come to an end, I invite you to join me in this prayer:

Jesus, I hear your words, and I am convicted. I see that you speak of me in this teaching from Matthew 7. Who among us hasn't noticed the speck in our brother's or sister's eye, even while we ignore a plank in our own eye? I've done this, Lord. I admit it. It's so easy to notice the faults in others and to ignore the faults in my own life. Forgive me.

Lord, protect me from hypocrisy. Give me the courage to stop excusing the sin in my own life. Lord, give me integrity. Give me the strength to remove the board from my own eye. And Lord, help me to be a person of mercy. Give me the love to share the transformation, new life, forgiveness, and freedom from sins that you offer. Jesus, you treated people not with condemnation but with integrity and mercy. Help me to learn from you. In your name. Amen.

DAY TWENTY-EIGHT

Thinking about My Relationships

Point to Ponder: I HAVE SINNED. I AM FORGIVEN.

Verse to Remember: *Mercy triumphs over judgment!* (James 2:13).

Question to Consider: Schedule a time to personally reflect on the questions in the "Self-Test" section on pages 239–41.

Tomorrow: The desire to be great

The Greatest
Are the Servants

The greatest among you will be your servant. For whoever exalts himself will be humbled, and whoever humbles himself will be exalted.

Matthew 23:11-12

29

The Desire
to Be Great

Walk in Jesus' sandals as you experience the truth his disciples discovered on their way to Jerusalem. Look for the relational twists as you read this story.

EXPERIENCE THE TRUTH

Any group of thirteen people doesn't normally walk together in one big bunch. Some forge ahead and some lag behind; some prefer to be alone with their thoughts and some like to talk in groups of three or four. This day, Jesus was walking out ahead of the disciples, and they fell back because of their fear. It took everything they had to follow Jesus on this journey.

They were headed toward Jerusalem, the center of religious and political power in Israel. Jesus had upset all of the power structures with his words and miracles — and now this group was walking right into the lions' den. Sensing their fear, Jesus took time on this walk to tell them about what would happen in Jerusalem. He was brutally and beautifully honest with them. "When we get to Jerusalem," Jesus said of himself, "the Son of Man will be betrayed to the leading priests and the teachers of religious law. They will sentence him to die and hand him over to the Romans. They will mock him, spit on him, beat him with their whips, and kill him, but after three days he will rise again."

Shocking! What would have been your response to this kind of statement? Jesus has just told you he is going to die. And then he tells you he is going to rise again in three days! It seems the natural response would be to begin to ask questions about what Jesus was facing: "Are you sure you have to die? What do you mean you'll rise again?"

But the disciples do not focus their attention on Jesus. Instead, in a surprising yet familiar relational twist, they focus on themselves! The brothers James and John start the parade. Right after Jesus tells them he is going to die, they approach Jesus and ask to sit in the top places of honor beside him. Instead of expressing compassion or even concern about the death Jesus has just told them he will face, they say something like, "Uh, we thought we heard something about thrones in what you just said, Jesus. Could we sit on the ones right next to you?" The other ten disciples catch wind of this request by James and John, and an argument breaks out:

"I deserve to sit next to Jesus!" "No you don't; I do."
"Not you; me!"

Amazingly, the only one who does not focus on himself is Jesus. Instead of getting angry at his disciples for not caring about his needs, he calls them aside to meet their needs. He knew their hearts. He understood that they were afraid. It's painful to see how quickly we become selfish when we're anxious or afraid. Jesus calmed his disciples' anxiety by refocusing their hearts. "You've observed how godless rulers throw their weight around," he said, "and when people get a little power how quickly it goes to their heads. It's not going to be that way with you. Whoever wants to be great must become a servant."

Based on Mark 10:32-45 (NLT, MSG)

If you want to have great relationships, don't miss what Jesus said about greatness: "Whoever wants to be great among you must be your servant" (Mark 10:43). The relationship principle is this: "The greatest are the servants."

Don't miss the strong connection between our desire to be great and our decision to humbly serve. It's easy to think that being humble means we pretend we don't have any desires for greatness. According to Jesus, nothing could be further from the truth. When his disciples expressed ambitions for greatness, Jesus didn't tell them to stop wanting to be great. Instead, he told them, "Anyone wanting to be the greatest must be the least—the servant of all!" (Mark 9:35 LB). We all have a desire for greatness, and Jesus taught us to translate our desires for greatness into actions of humility. He taught us to translate our desire to be significant into a decision to serve. When you learn how to plug this truth into your life, it will result in the greatest relationships possible—and the greatest life possible!

Because it can be difficult to see this connection, many people never strive toward the humility that will make them truly great—the humility that would cause them to make an immeasurable impact on the world, to build a marriage that shines like a light in this world, to make them the kind of parent so needed in this world.

> *In every relationship we face this same test: Will I exalt myself, or will I humble myself?*

This was far from the only time Jesus talked to his disciples about true greatness coming through the path of service. It was a constant theme of his teaching. Jesus often followed his statements about becoming great through serving with what I like to call his "daily greatness quiz." Jesus stated it this way: "Whoever exalts himself will be humbled, and whoever humbles himself will be exalted" (Matthew 23:12).

Every day we face a simple test of greatness:

☐ I will exalt myself.
☐ I will humble myself.

Check one!

In every relationship we face this same test: Will I exalt myself, or will I humble myself? Choose one. In decisions ranging from the career path you take to the car you buy to even the clothes you wear, this test is in front of you daily. From the grandest dreams to the simplest details, you take this test of greatness each and every day.

- Who will be the first to apologize after an argument?
- How will I respond to this problem as a parent?
- Can I handle this disagreement with my friend?
- Who gets the remote control?
- Will I exalt myself, or will I humble myself?
  Choose one, because you can't choose both.

Humility is at the core of any strong relationship. The truth is, we cannot have good and growing relationships if we're not humble. It's absolutely impossible. Why? Because selfishness destroys relationships, and humility develops relationships. I need the foundation of humility at my core to put aside the selfishness that will erode any relationship.

Some people think this choice to humble or exalt lies solely with God: he lifts me up, or he lets me down. God humbles me, or God exalts me. Jesus taught, "Whoever humbles himself will be exalted." "Humbles *himself*" points to a choice I must make. It is God's choice how he will respond to our humility—and, as Jesus tells us, God chooses to *exalt* those who humble themselves.

How can you be great at being humble? Sounds like a contradiction, doesn't it? Reminds you of the preacher who said, "I have a great sermon on humility—probably the best you've ever heard!" Jesus told us, "Whoever exalts himself will be humbled; whoever humbles himself will be exalted." For the next four days we're going to unpack this statement and see how humility makes for great relationships in four specific life challenges—your ambitions, your need to be noticed, your tendency to compare, and your relationship with God. It's going to be a great week as we focus on what Jesus taught about true greatness.

DAY TWENTY-NINE

Thinking about My Relationships

Point to Ponder: Jesus teaches us to translate our desire for greatness into actions of humility.

Verse to Remember: *"Whoever exalts himself will be humbled, and whoever humbles himself will be exalted"* (Matthew 23:12).

Question to Consider: Is there some way my concept of humility needs to change?

Tomorrow: How humility handles ambition

30

How Humility
Handles Ambition

Is it wrong to have ambitions? Of course not. Look at some of the great examples of faith in the Bible. Did Abraham have ambition? He had an ambition to go to a land where God was sending him, and because of his response God calls him the father of our faith (see Romans 4:11). Did Noah have ambition? It took more than a little ambition to build an ark that took over one hundred years to complete! Did David have any ambition? How else would he have confronted and defeated Goliath? How about Jesus himself? He set his face to go to Jerusalem because that's where the Father was sending him (see Luke 9:51). He made it his holy ambition to complete the Father's plan.

There are three reasons everyone should have great ambitions:

- *We are created by God.* God has ambitions for all of his creation. His ambition is that every part of creation lives out the purpose for which it was fashioned.

- *We are given responsibility over this world.* God gave us this mandate: "Fill the earth and subdue it. Rule over the fish of the sea and the birds of the air and over every living creature that moves on the ground" (Genesis 1:28). We're given responsibility to manage the world—a very big and ambitious job!
- *We are made to reflect God's image in this world.* This is amazingly ambitious. Not only did God create us and make us responsible for the world he made; he also made us to reflect his image in the world.

A God-given ambition is an ambition that grows out of these three truths. If you have a plan or idea that grows out of the humble recognition that you are God's creation who is given responsibility for this world and desires to reflect his image, go for it! You have found the fertile ground from which God-given ambitions grow. We need more godly ambition in this world.

It's not wrong to have ambition; it's wrong to have *selfish* ambitions. The problem isn't that we're ambitious; the problem is that we often allow pride to drive our ambition rather than choosing to let humility manage our ambitions.

Who Is the Greatest in the Kingdom?

The subject of greatness seems to have been a favorite topic among Jesus' disciples. Think of what Jesus faced every day. He was empowering these men to change the world, and they always seemed to be lagging five steps behind, saying among themselves, "I'm better than you are." Jesus must have often wondered, "*They're* going to change the world?" Of course, with divine insight, he knew there was far more in them than was apparent on the surface. So he taught them about how humility could manage their ambition, even as they argued about which one of them was the greatest.

Matthew tells of Jesus' bringing a child into the disciples' midst to paint a powerful picture. Pointing to the child, Jesus declared, "Whoever humbles himself like this child is the greatest in the kingdom of heaven" (Matthew 18:4). Jesus challenges them to learn about true greatness from a child. Jesus talks to disciples who are demanding to get their own way, and he uses the example of a child who must depend on others.

> Demand or depend — this is the choice we make each day.

Remember the daily greatness quiz? Will I exalt myself, or will I humble myself. One way to exalt yourself is to demand your own way; to humble yourself is to depend on someone else. Demand or depend — this is the choice we make each day. Either we demand our way, our rights, our due, or we depend on God.

Have you noticed how easy it is to be demanding? I sure have! It appears an attractive option because it seems to be effective in getting us what we want. As we look around, we see that those who are most demanding often seem to get the quickest results. Demand that your order be changed in a restaurant — and most of the time the waiter will rush to your aid and bring you want you want. Go into a store and demand service — and you get what you want. I was in a store recently, and a customer walked into an aisle and yelled at the top of her lungs, "Clerk!" Sales associates rushed to help her. For her — and often for us — demanding seems to work just fine.

You might possibly demand your way to business success or even demand your way to greater wealth. But here is the problem: you cannot demand the most important things. You can't demand yourself to be happy. You can't demand that you are never going to get sick, that you will never die. You cannot demand a relationship to work. You may have tried, but you can't demand that someone love you.

Demanding is tricky—and even dangerous. While it sometimes gets you the little things, it can keep you from the most important things. You demand this, you demand that; you get this, you get that. But then you demand to have something important. You demand a relationship that's breaking apart to come back together, but nothing happens. So you demand harder—but it pushes you further apart, and you wonder what's wrong. Did the rules change? Why isn't the demanding working like it used to work? The rules didn't change. It's just that while you can demand little things, *you cannot demand the most important things.* Demanding will fool you; it seems to get you what you want quickly, but in the long run it will have the opposite effect, and you will lose everything you so fervently dreamed of having.

Unless You Become Like Children

What can we learn from a child about the kind of humility that manages our ambitions? Children have different facial features and backgrounds and personalities, but at the core they all have one thing in common: they have to depend on someone else—on their parents and other adults in their lives.

Have you noticed that most children are totally fine with

this arrangement? They don't agonize over asking their parents for things. A child doesn't think for days or weeks, "Should I ask them, or shouldn't I? Will it depress them, or will it make them angry if I ask them?" In fact, most children don't think about it at all. Instead, they see their parents as the source for meeting all their needs. I saw a guy walking down the street the other day with his three kids. He was wearing a T-shirt that read, "Do I look like an ATM machine?" For his children, the answer is, "Yes!" Our children don't mind asking, because they know they must depend on us. God created you to live in that same kind of relationship with him.

Give yourself to the greater ambition of God's plan — a plan that begins with childlike dependence.

You may be thinking, "But I had a hard time asking when I was a child." Difficult circumstances or angry words made it seem you were always asking for too much. If this is what you experienced, you may well have a hard time asking God to meet all your needs. Jesus tells us that in a healthy relationship, those who depend ask for help from those they depend on: "Ask and it will be given to you; seek and you will find; knock and the door will be opened to you" (Matthew 7:7). *Ask!* Make the decision to depend on God. Jesus asked a child to stand among his disciples so he could teach them to depend on him like children — to reach out to him with a childlike faith and to not be afraid to ask him for anything.

Jesus taught that choosing a humble attitude of dependence cannot happen without change: "Unless you change and become like little children" (Matthew 18:3). Humility means you change your choice from demanding your own way to depending on God.

God loves you—he made you. God has a plan for your life—he made you responsible. God desires to show his love through your life—he made you responsible in order to reflect his image. With these assurances in mind, you don't have to go through life demanding your way. Humility doesn't mean you let go of your ambitions; it means you give yourself to the greater ambition of God's plan—a plan that begins with childlike dependence. True greatness is depending on God.

DAY THIRTY
Thinking about My Relationships

Point to Ponder: True greatness is depending on God.

Verse to Remember: *"Whoever humbles himself like this child is the greatest in the kingdom of heaven"* (Matthew 18:4).

Question to Consider: Am I demanding something of myself or others for which I should be depending on God?

Tomorrow: How humility handles our need to be noticed

31

How Humility Handles Our Need to Be Noticed

Our relationships are filled with the need for notice. If you are a parent, look at your kids. Do they ever compete for your attention? My wife and I have three children, and when they were younger, it was almost impossible to take a picture of just one of our children. The others always tried to get in the picture. They wanted to be noticed. And it's not just kids who strive to be noticed. As husband and wife, do you ever play the "It's My Turn to Be Noticed Today" game?

We all enjoy being noticed. But it's all too easy for this enjoyment to turn into a need—to become a relational drug. You can get addicted to the need to be noticed to the extent that, in order to feel important, you have to have it every day.

With the choice to humble yourself, you begin to see the world differently. Instead of always needing to be noticed by others, you begin to notice others' needs. You're no longer the sole focus of your soul's attention. You find a refreshing freedom to see, care about, and act on the needs you see around you.

Let's join Jesus and his followers to listen in on what he had to say about this. As we pick up the story, remember that the disciples have a real issue among themselves about who's at the top of the heap and who's the most noticed — about who's going to be closest to Jesus when they get to heaven.

One of the ways Jesus teaches his disciples about humility is to point to the religious leaders of his day: "Do not do what they do.... Everything they do is done for men to see" (Matthew 23:3, 5). They needed others' notice. They were very religious men, but every religious action grew out of their need to be noticed. Jesus reserved his most scathing words for these leaders. He knew they were using religion as a cover for getting their needs for notice met. He also knew everyone was looking at them as a model — and it was a model Jesus did *not* want his disciples to adopt in their lives.

Jesus gave his disciples a list of three things that served as a telltale sign of their need to be noticed: "They make their phylacteries wide ...; they love the place of honor at banquets ...; they love to ... have men call them 'Rabbi'" (Matthew 23:5–7). It's a good list of the methods we still use today in our attempts to get noticed.

They Make Their Phylacteries Wide

A *phylactery* sounds like something you'd find in a natural history museum. You can almost hear a nasal-voiced museum guide saying, "In this exhibit we have the fossil remains of the pterodactyl and the phylactery."

A phylactery was a little box worn on the head that contained Scripture verses. It was intended to honor the Old Testament teaching to carry God's word with you throughout the day. Pride had crept into the use of these phylacteries. One Pharisee would make his Bible box a bit bigger than the next Pharisee's Bible box—showing he had more of the Bible on his mind. Then the next guy would make his box a bit bigger than the other guy's box. And the phylacteries got wider and wider. You can imagine these Pharisees walking around with warehouse boxes on their head because they were so spiritual!

The phylactery is a perfect picture of our love of symbols. When we are caught up in the need to be noticed, we begin to love symbols. We look at these ancient religious leaders and think, "How ridiculous that they wore boxes on their heads!" We're not anything like that today, are we? We are so much more sophisticated. We walk around with little logos on our shirts in order to feel important, not boxes on our heads. We are much more spiritual than they were. We buy a car with the symbol we've been looking all of our lives to be able to afford. Then we drive around thinking that everybody in the world is noticing us because we're driving around with that symbol on our car. "They probably all want to be like me," we think. It is the love of symbols.

I honestly don't think God cares about what logo is on your clothes or insists you buy the lowest model car. You don't have to drive a Hyundai to be holy. But God does care about *why* you drive the model of car you drive. He does care about *why* you wear the kind of clothes you wear. He does care about *why* you live in the kind of house you live in. Jesus told us to watch out that we don't arrange everything in our lives around the need to be noticed. This need can become so all-consuming that it has the potential to rip apart even your most important relationships.

They Love the Place of Honor at Banquets

Those who need to be noticed not only have a love of symbols; they also have a love of recognition and honor. For these religious leaders, it meant making sure they had a place at the head table at the banquet — the place where others could look at them and think, "He must be important; look at where he is sitting."

We can fall in love with head tables also. We all like to see our name in the program, to hear our name mentioned, to receive the honors that let others know we've worked hard. The most popular Google Internet search is to search for your own name to see if it comes up first. This natural interest in ourselves can easily turn into a love of honor. We get to a place where we *must* see our name in the program, we *expect* to hear our name mentioned, and the potential honor becomes the *very reason* we work hard. If you've ever had an evening ruined because your name was never mentioned, you understand this love of honor.

They Love to Have Men Call Them "Rabbi"

Out of our need to be noticed grow a love of symbols, a love of honor and recognition, and, finally, a love of titles. It wasn't enough to *be* a teacher; these religious leaders of Jesus' day wanted to hear people *call* them "Teacher."

There's nothing inherently wrong with titles, and titles can help let others know about our responsibilities. Remember that a title is only important in that it expresses your ability to serve others. If I began experiencing chest pains on an airplane, I would be thrilled to have the person next to me say, "I'm Dr. John Jones; how can I help?" Titles can be an expression of a willingness to serve.

Yet these same titles that express our desire to serve can become something we love for the notice they bring. How do you know if you're in love with your title? You *have* to hear it! Hearing your title makes you feel important, so the more often you can hear it, the better.

Noticing the Needs of Others

To exalt yourself means you need to be noticed by others. It's a need that is never fulfilled. If you go down that road, you'll find that the more notice you get, the more you need. You can make a different choice. You can choose to humble yourself and to notice others' needs. The only way to be cured of this need to be noticed is to start noticing other people's needs.

In a poem titled "I Wonder," Ruth Harms Calkin asked a heart-searching question:

> *You know, Lord, how I serve you*
> *With great emotional fervor in the limelight.*
> *You know how eagerly I speak for you at a Women's Club.*
> *You know my genuine enthusiasm at a Bible study.*
> *But how would I react, I wonder,*
> *If you pointed to a basin of water*
> *And asked me to wash the calloused feet*
> *Of a bent and wrinkled old woman*
> *Day after day, month after month,*
> *In a room where nobody saw and nobody knew?**

---

*Quoted in Charles R. Swindoll, *Improving Your Serve* (Nashville: Nelson, 2004), 34–35.

That's a humility question—and so is this one: "Am I serving because I need to be noticed or because I notice and want to meet others' needs?" I don't know about you, but for me this poem probes at some tender spots. I enjoy being noticed when I serve. I'm often reminded of what C. S. Lewis said about humility: "If anyone would like to acquire humility I can, I think, tell him the first step. The first step is to realize that one is proud."* The ugly but clear truth about me is, I am proud. We all have to deal with pride in our lives. There is a place in all of us—sometimes a big place—that would rather have our needs noticed than notice others' needs. The key to great relationships is to let Jesus Christ turn this preference in us upside down.

Our need for notice is a real thing. So how do we set aside this need to focus on the needs of others? Here's the only answer: Trust God to meet your need for notice! Immerse yourself in the truth that God has promised to meet your needs. Paul exudes this confidence: "My God will use his wonderful riches in Christ Jesus to give you everything you need" (Philippians 4:19 NCV). God doesn't give us everything we want, but he does give us everything we need. Trust him, even when he doesn't give you what you *want*, and keep asking him for what you *need*. This confidence that God will meet your needs gives you a new freedom to be able to notice and meet others' needs.

God will meet your need for recognition. He understands you have this need. He notices you now in ways beyond your ability to see. One day, he will notice you in a way you can't help but see. On that day, those who love him will stand

---

*C. S. Lewis, *Mere Christianity* (New York: Macmillan, 1981), 108.

before him, and he will look at us individually, personally, lovingly, and say, "Well done, good and faithful servant." When you hear these words, the notice from others you've chased after all your life will pale to nothing in comparison. He alone can and *will* meet all of your needs.

Choose to notice others' needs—not just the needs of your friends, but the needs of that person at the grocery store who irritates you by standing in your way and squeezing every peach in the bin, or the sales associate who seems a little slow, or the person in the office cubicle next to you who has turned into your sworn enemy!

Immerse yourself in the truth that God has promised to meet your needs.

Maybe your coworker has his music turned up just loud enough to really bug you. Every time he gets up to go to the bathroom, you want to sneak into his office and bend all the paper clips into pretzel shapes. What if this week you decide to notice the fact that he has some needs? What if when you go to get a Coke, you bring him one too? Don't say, "I'll give you this Coke, but you'll have to turn the music down." Just give it to him as an expression of kindness. Notice the fact that he has needs, and begin treating him like a human being. It will do him some good, to be sure, and, just as important, it will do *you* some good. When you start to meet others' needs, you will see your own stress level go down. One small kindness will have more impact than you can possibly imagine. Mother Teresa once said, "We have an opportunity to love others as he loves us, not in big things, but in small things with great love."[*] A

---

[*]Quoted in Kathryn Spink, *Mother Teresa: A Complete Authorized Biography* (New York: HarperCollins, 1997), 169.

life focused on yourself and the meeting of your own needs will never be a great life, because it can get no larger than just you. Every great life is focused on meeting other people's needs.

DAY THIRTY-ONE

Thinking about My Relationships

Point to Ponder: The only way to be cured of the need to be noticed is to begin noticing other people's needs.

Verse to Remember: *Be devoted to one another in brotherly love. Honor one another above yourselves* (Romans 12:10).

Question to Consider: What seemingly small need can I meet for someone else today?

Tomorrow: How humility handles our tendency to compare

32

How Humility Handles
Our Tendency to Compare

Because we equate being first with being greatest, we are always comparing. Every room we walk into, every business meeting we attend, every conversation we have, we find ourselves asking where we stand: Am I ahead, or am I behind? Am I above, or am I below?

This tendency to compare has an immeasurable impact on our relationships. The comparison trap can ruin even the best of relationships. What you have is good, yet you start looking around and comparing: "He seems more attentive than my husband." "She encourages me even more than my wife does." "Look at those kids. Why can't my children behave that well?" Satan tempts us to take something good and compare the joy right out of it. The truth is, you don't know how that attentive guy treats his family at home; you don't know how often that encouraging woman loves to gossip with her girlfriends; you don't see those other kids when they're on a sugar high.

EXPERIENCE THE TRUTH

Jesus was a people watcher. One day, as people walked into a dinner party, Jesus observed them milling around near the most coveted seats. The tables were set up in a U-shape. The head table for the host and his important guests was at the top of the U. Down the sides sat the less honored persons at the party. As people waited to take their seats, they assessed the importance of everyone else in the room: "I'm better than he is, more important than he is, higher on the scale than she is. It looks like I deserve to have that top spot." People started sitting as close to the top spot as they thought they deserved — musical chairs for social climbers.

Based on what he saw at this party, Jesus shared some relational advice: "When someone invites you to a wedding feast, do not take the place of honor, for a person more distinguished than you may have been invited. If so, the host who invited both of you will come and say to you, 'Give this man your seat.' Then, humiliated, you will have to take the least important place. But when you are invited, take the lowest place, so that when your host comes, he will say to you, 'Friend, move up to a better place.' Then you will be honored in the presence of all your fellow guests. For everyone who exalts himself will be humbled, and he who humbles himself will be exalted."

Based on Luke 14:7-14

Principle #5: The Greatest Are the Servants

Jesus reminds us that we face a daily greatness quiz in this area of comparison: Will I exalt myself and try to get the first place, or will I humble myself and decide to take the lowest seat?

In most of the world today, we equate being first with being greatest. First place, first string, first chair, first class — all expressions of what is thought to be the greatest and best. Jesus taught us that greatness is not a matter of winning a competition; greatness is a matter of humbly living the life God gave you to live. And God is much more concerned with who you're helping in the race than who you're ahead of. He's not asking, "Will you get to the finish line before anyone else?" He is asking, "Who are you going to help cross the finish line with you?"

Do you humble yourself by taking the lowest place? To me, this is one of life's most challenging questions. The amazing thing is that Jesus didn't just say, "Be satisfied if you're *given* the lowest seat"; he said, "*Take* the lowest place." Making the decision to take the lowest place is very different from tolerating your placement in the lowest seat.

I have to tell you, I would be more than happy to take the lowest place *as long as* I knew someone was likely going to tap me on the shoulder and say, "You're in the wrong seat, sir. Come on up and sit at the highest spot." But what if I take the lowest place — and I have to stay there? What if I see someone who I think is less important than I am sitting in a higher place than I'm sitting in? Will I find myself thinking, "What in the world am I doing down here when they are sitting up there?"

As we grow in spiritual maturity, we typically go through three phases as we consider which spot to seek. In phase one

I'm ruled by selfishness, and so I strive for the top spot. I may do it in obvious ways or in subtle ways, but in my mind I strive to sit in the top spot. I'm convinced it will make me feel important.

As I grow in humility, I reach phase two. I take the lower spot, hoping it will get me to the top spot. It's my seemingly unselfish path to the top spot. Many of us live the bulk of our lives at this second phase. We act unselfishly, hoping it will get us what we selfishly wanted all along.

Often in what seems to be the lowest spot we find life's greatest blessings.

There is a third phase, where we are equally comfortable in the bottom spot or the top spot. We've realized it doesn't really matter who we think is first. At this level, if you're in the lowest spot you think, "If I'm here, God can use me here. There may be somebody sitting next to me I wouldn't be talking to if I was up there. There may be somebody who could talk to me here and make a difference I would never see happen if I were sitting somewhere else. God can use me right here." But there is more to it. When I reach this phase, I also realize that if I happen to end up in the highest spot, God can also use me there. You're able to say to yourself, "He wants to work in and through me here. Who is it I need to talk to here? There is something God wants to do in my life in this spot." You are equally satisfied, no matter where God happens to put you.

I haven't reached this third stage yet. I hope to get there someday. I really do want to be there. Every once in a while, I have a brief experience of the freedom that would be mine if I were constantly there. I don't want to be so concerned about comparing and competing that it eats away my passion for what is truly important.

Here's the beautiful surprise God brings: it's often in what seems to be the lowest spot that we find life's greatest blessings. The richest relationships, the purest joys, the most profound influences are often found when we are out of the limelight and feel free to simply love and serve. F. B. Meyer put it this way: "I used to think that God's gifts were on shelves, one above the other, and the taller we grew in Christian character, the more easily we could reach them. I now find that God's gifts are on shelves, one beneath the other; and it is not a question of growing taller, but of stooping lower."[*]

If you are someone who lives for the thrill of competition, you're probably thinking, "This is crazy. Does the Bible really say that?" If you are motivated by healthy competition, God is not telling you to deny the way you were made. If you are wired for competition, be competitive — but be competitive about something different from what most competitive people settle for. Be competitive about something different from you *being first*! Six and a half billion people in the world, and the highest goal you can think of is you being in first place? Not a very lofty goal! If God wired you to be competitive, be competitive about feeding people who are starving. I'm not saying to compete with other people who are trying to help. Compete with the enemy called starvation. You're built to be competitive, so be competitive about taking the good news about Jesus' love to places in the world no one else will go. Be competitive about being the best husband, best wife, best

---

[*]Quoted in Paul W. Powell, *The Night Cometh* (Waco, Tex.: self-published, 2002), 33.

mom, best dad you can be. Be competitive about things that are truly important.

God is faithful to use those who stop worrying about who is the greatest. He is able to change the world through those who say, "God, wherever you put me, I'm going to do something that makes a difference for you in the world today." This is Jesus' path to true greatness. This is how humility handles this tendency we have to compare ourselves to others and to fight for the highest place.

DAY THIRTY-TWO
Thinking about My Relationships

Point to Ponder: Jesus didn't just say, "Be satisfied if you're given the lowest seat"; he said, "*Take* the lowest place."

Verse to Remember: *We do not dare to classify or compare ourselves with some who commend themselves. When they measure themselves by themselves and compare themselves with themselves, they are not wise* (2 Corinthians 10:12).

Questions to Consider: Have I ever been willing to take the lowest place? When I did, what happened?

Tomorrow: How humility handles our relationship with God

33

How Humility Handles Our Relationship with God

EXPERIENCE THE TRUTH

Jesus told a simple story about two men who prayed two very different prayers. The first man was a Pharisee, at the height of religious respect in his culture, and the second was a tax collector, at the bottom rung of respectability. Tax collectors were hated because they cooperated with the Roman occupation of Israel. The gap couldn't have been wider between these two men. They happen to come into a place of worship at the same time — to say prayers on opposite sides of the room. The Pharisee prays, "God, I thank you I'm not like other men — robbers, evildoers, adulterers — or even like that tax collector over there. I fast twice a week and give a tenth of all I get." The tax collector prays a much shorter prayer: "God, have mercy on me. I'm a sinner."

One prayer was a commentary, the other a confession. The first prayer focused on impressing God, the second on expressing a need. One man prayed, "Look at me"; the other prayed, "Forgive me." One prayed, "I have God's blessing"; the other prayed, "I need God's mercy."

Underlying Jesus' parable is the question, "Whose prayer do you think God heard?" Whatever your preconceptions about Pharisees or tax collectors may be, the answer is obvious: God heard the honest prayer. Jesus said of the tax collector, "I tell you that this man, rather than the other, went home justified before God. For everyone who exalts himself will be humbled, and he who humbles himself will be exalted."

Based on Luke 18:9-14

How does humility handle the personal relationship we have with God? Let's remind ourselves of our daily greatness quiz: Will I exalt myself, or will I humble myself?

When you exalt yourself, you end up with a *do-it-yourself* design for relating to God. It's all up to you. It is no accident that this Pharisee, who was immersed in religion, had fallen into the do-it-yourself trap — a trap you may be more prone to fall into the longer you hang around church. What started out as a fresh dependence on God can slide into a less challenging reliance on yourself. "After all," you think, "I've made progress on this 'faith thing.' God, I think I've got it figured out now. I'll take it from here." All of a sudden, you're depending on yourself.

No one ever intends to become a Pharisee. This Pharisee didn't wake up one day and think, "In my pursuit of God, I'd like to get as far away from him as possible, so I'm going to build rules into my life that ruin my heart for him." He just slid into it, step by step, rule by rule, condemnation of others by condemnation of others. We can slide there too—maybe you already have. Jesus' simple story about the Pharisee and the tax collector serves to encourage us to break out of the discouragement of a do-it-yourself life.

In this story, Jesus pointed to the signs of do-it-yourself religion. These can serve as warning signs for all of us, showing us that we are moving from depending on God to doing it ourselves:

- *You become confident in yourself.* The feeling begins to creep into the back of your mind that God is fortunate to have you as a follower.
- *You become condemning of others.* Whenever you quickly and easily fall into the trap of condemning others, you give evidence that you're depending on yourself.
- *You become content with externals.* "I fast ... and give a tenth." It's not that there is anything wrong with these externals; it's that they are all that's left. You've become content with the trappings of religion.

The solution to the do-it-yourself trap is to *trust in God.* The night before Jesus died, he knew his followers were anxious. They were confused about exactly what was going to happen, but they knew that somehow everything was about to change. As we all do when facing an uncertain future, they worried. Jesus looked them in the eye and said, "Do not let your hearts be troubled. Trust in God; trust also in me" (John 14:1). That's simple! Trust in God. The Greek word for "troubled" paints the picture of water being stirred up, as on a stormy sea. *When the storm hits, trust in God.*

I remember the storm I faced when my mother was in the last stages of cancer. She lived about a two-hour drive by car from the town where I lived. Once a week or so, I would drive through the valley and over the curvy mountain roads to spend a few hours with her. Although her tenacious spirit never allowed her to admit it, we all knew she didn't have long to live. She was a believer in Jesus Christ, and I knew she was headed for an eternity of joy in heaven. However, I was unprepared for the waves of emotion that would hit me as I watched her slipping away, the wave of her body growing weaker, the wave of her mind becoming confused and agitated. I felt drenched by the realities of her illness. Oh, I wanted her to be with the Lord, but not this soon and not like this. Everything in me wanted to do something to stop this. So I got on the do-it-yourself road. Frantically, I chased after ways to stop what was happening to my mother. I found myself constantly doing things to try to ease my own hurting—regardless of whether it had anything to do with my mom. (I'm not saying we shouldn't do all we possibly can for someone we love. My activities, however, were often nothing more than pointless exertion of energy.)

When the storm hits, trust in God.

One night as I was driving home after seeing her, weariness overwhelmed me. As I rounded one dark curve after another, I was struck again and again by the thought, "How can I possibly help my mother when I don't even have the strength to face the fact that she is dying?" At that very moment, I recalled Jesus' words: "Come to me, all you who are weary and burdened, and I will give you rest" (Matthew 11:28).

"I will give you rest!" The experience of these words coming into my mind was so powerful and personal that I could almost sense Jesus riding with me in that car. In the perfect timing of God, I rounded the last curve through the mountains and saw the expanse and the lights of the valley spread out in front of me. The thought hit me that God wanted to broaden my perspective, to help me grow more aware of the fact that he is working, even when I can't. I must have repeated those words—"I will give you rest"—hundreds of times to myself during the weeks leading up to my mother's death. The hurt was real, but God's promise made his presence and strength just as real. His promise calmed the storm in my heart as I faced the death of my mother.

Jesus understands the storms that rage in your heart. He says to you, "Don't let your heart be troubled. Trust! Trust in God; trust also in me."

Thinking about My Relationships

Point to Ponder: Your relationship with God is either growing in trust or sliding toward do-it-yourself religion.

Verse to Remember: *"Come to me, all you who are weary and burdened, and I will give you rest"* (Matthew 11:28).

Question to Consider: How do I need to confess my needs in prayer and depend on God to meet my needs today?

Tomorrow: Vine and branches

34

Vine and Branches

All this talk about humble greatness is difficult for many of
us. Some have been so intent on greatness that humility is
the last thing on their minds; others have been so focused
on humility that any thoughts of greatness seem somehow
wrong. Our minds beg for a picture of what humility and
greatness look like in the same frame. Thankfully, Jesus gives
us such a picture in John 15, where he teaches about the vine
and the branches.

Jesus knew how to make things astonishingly, profoundly
simple. He said, "I am the vine; you are the branches" (verse
5). It's a simple picture, communicating the two things we
need to remember each day if we're going to live the great
life God intends for us: he's the vine; we're the branches.
God doesn't intend for you to live a burdensome life—one
where your relationships are spinning out of control or where
you're constantly feeling, "I'd love to accomplish more, but
I'm just not doing what God wants me to." He wants you to
live a great life. Jesus uses a powerful image to describe the

satisfying, significant life he intends for you to live — *bear fruit*. No one has a problem-free life, but Jesus intends for all of us to live a fruitful life. This life starts with remembering two things: I am a branch, and Jesus is the vine.

I Am a Branch

Great people have a good handle on who they are. It's one of the keys to being fruitful in life. In John 15, Jesus compares our lives to a vineyard. God is the gardener, Jesus is the vine, and we are the branches. Some believe that a grape vineyard is the most difficult of all agricultural pursuits. It takes more constant care and more hard work than any other type of agriculture. Much to our relief, that's not our worry! God is the gardener, not you. God is the one who provides that care. God is the one who tends your life.

Jesus is the vine. The vine draws life-giving and fruit-bearing strength from the soil to give to the branches. Jesus is where you find the life you need. Have you ever tried letting anything else be your vine besides Jesus Christ? We've all pursued joy and purpose somewhere else. Jesus longs for us to remember this simple truth: He is the only place to find life. He is the way, the truth, and the life. He is the vine.

You are a branch. What is the job of a branch? The branch must *stay attached* to the vine. In a nutshell, that sums it up. When the branch stays attached, it will be kept under the constant care of the gardener and enabled to draw life from the vine. You are dependent on the vine. The vine is where life and growth and fruitfulness are found.

I am a branch. That's who I am. If you're like me, you have to remind yourself of that reality every day. As a branch, your calling is to fulfill God's desire for you to be fruitful. What is the fruit? The branch reproduces the life that's in the vine. The fruit is *being like Jesus Christ*—not just in your thoughts but also in your actions. The more you become like Jesus Christ, the more fruitful your life is. The vine gives life to the branch.

One important warning before we move on: You are a branch that God expects to be fruitful, and in order to be fruitful, branches must be pruned. If I don't understand pruning, I'm going to be confused for the rest of my life. It'll look like God's doing great things in my life and I'm growing—and then all of a sudden there'll be a *snip*! "God, why did you do that? That was my best-looking offshoot! It had great leaves on it."

Vines need drastic pruning to continue to be fruitful. The gardener will cut off 90 to 95 percent of a grapevine in pruning. Pruning hurts. There's no pruning without pain. But in the pain there is the promise of greater fruit.

I grew up in northern California in an area called "the wine country." You couldn't drive for five minutes without passing a grape vineyard. In summertime, the vineyards were green and luxurious, and as the grapes began to form, the branches were fruitful. In the fall, the vineyards were even more beautiful as the leaves on the vines turned regal red and gold. In early springtime, the vineyards were ugly. The leaves had fallen off, the branches had been pruned, and the vineyard was row after row of bare sticks.

> The more you become like Jesus Christ, the more fruitful your life is.

It may be springtime in the vineyard of your life right now. You look at your life and say, "It's just a bunch of ugly, bare sticks! What's God doing in my life?" He's been pruning. The fruit will come. Yes, it hurts to be pruned, but God is more interested in your growth than your comfort. God has been pruning you. Through his Word, through relationships, through circumstances, he has been pruning you. You are a branch, and the gardener is at work to make you the most fruitful branch possible.

Jesus Is the Vine

Jesus is where true life is to be found. He told us that we as the branches must *abide* in the vine. The word *abide* (or *remain*) appears ten times in the first eleven verses of John 15. Jesus wanted to make sure we saw the necessity of abiding and trusting in him.

What does *abide* mean? The answer is simple when we remember that we're talking about a vine and its branches. To abide is to be *attached*. Jesus is saying, "Stay 100 percent attached to me." Some people make the word *abide* complicated, adding all kinds of levels of definition to try to get at its different possible meanings. Jesus boiled it down to its simplest expression: "I'm the vine; you're the branch — so abide in me, stay attached to me." How long can a branch live unattached to the vine? Not for a single moment. The branch needs the vine *all the time.*

Jesus doesn't intend this truth to be difficult to understand. "Read my Word," he tells us. "Make it a part of your life. Talk to me, and make me a part of every day. Thank me for the things in your life." These are the choices through which you abide. These habits mean nothing if you practice them in isolation; the significance is that they cause you to stay attached to the vine.

Without love, you cannot stay attached to the power and presence of Jesus in your daily life.

As important as these devotional habits are in staying connected to Jesus, there is something that is even more important. There is a deep connection between abiding in Christ and love. Don't miss this truth. It is absolutely vital to living the relationship principles discussed throughout this book. Jesus said, "Just as the Father has loved Me, I have also loved you; abide in My love. If you keep My commandments, you will abide in My love.... This is My commandment, that you love one another, just as I have loved you" (John 15:9–10, 12 NASB). If I keep Jesus' commandments, I will abide in, remain in, stay attached to his love. And what is the command that Jesus focuses on in these verses? It is the command to love—to love one another in response to his love for us. Wow! Without love, there is no possibility of staying attached to the power and presence of Jesus in your daily life. With love, Jesus guarantees that connection.

You cannot have a Christian marriage without abiding in Christ—you can be a Christian and married, but you can't have a Christ-honoring, Christ-centered, Christlike marriage without depending on him. You cannot run a Christian business without abiding in Christ. You cannot be a Christian parent without abiding in Christ. You cannot carry out a Christian ministry without abiding in Christ. You cannot be a Christian friend without abiding in Christ. You can try—but you'll end up tired and frustrated. "Abide in me," Jesus urged, "and I will abide in you. Then you will bear fruit for me." This fruit is not some temporary notoriety or fleeting achievement, but it is fruit that has eternal impact and lasting joy.

Apart from Jesus Christ you can't bear fruit in your life. You can't become like Christ apart from Christ. It's an empty and burdensome pursuit. On the other hand, when you do abide in Christ, you cannot help but bear fruit in your life. It's what a branch does when it is attached to the vine.

DAY THIRTY-FOUR
Thinking about My Relationships

Point to Ponder: I am a branch.

Verse to Remember: *"Yes, I am the vine; you are the branches. Those who remain in me, and I in them, will produce much fruit. For apart from me you can do nothing"* (John 15:5 NLT).

Question to Consider: Have I been viewing God's work in my life as punishing me when in reality he has been pruning me?

Tomorrow: The daily decision of humility

Principle #5: The Greatest Are the Servants

35

The Daily Decision
of Humility

Humility is a daily quiz: Will I exalt myself, or will I humble myself? We face this test with our ambitions and our need to be noticed, with our tendency to compare, and with our relationship with God. If you're to choose humility, it begins with how you think about humility. Many assume that humility has to do primarily with how you think about yourself. It does not. You're not going to arrive at humility by focusing on yourself. Humility has more to do with how you think about others and how you think about God.

Humility Is the Daily Decision
to Think of Others as More Important
Than Yourself

Philippians 2 is one of those chapters of the Bible you feel you should walk through on tiptoe in hushed tones. It is a holy place. The description of the humility that Jesus chose through his death on the cross is spiritually breathtaking:

Who, being in very nature God,
    did not consider equality with God something
        to be grasped,
but made himself nothing,
    taking the very nature of a servant,
    being made in human likeness.
And being found in appearance as a man,
    he humbled himself
    and became obedient to death—
        even death on a cross!

Philippians 2:6-8

As awe-inspiring as these words are, even more amazing to me are the words that precede these verses. Verse 5 reads, "Your attitude should be the same as that of Christ Jesus." The picture of Jesus as a humble servant is not meant to be a beautiful portrait to admire on the wall; it is meant to be a model that inspires us to act with humility.

Verse 3 of Philippians 2 (CEV) reads, "Don't be jealous or proud, but be humble and consider others more important than yourselves." That's the opposite of the way most of us think. We usually "consider ourselves more important than others." Be sure to notice that the Bible does not say to think of yourself as less important but to think of others as more important. To think of others as more important means you put into action the words that follow: "Each of you should look not only to your own interests, but also to the interests of others (verse 4).

Paul begins the discussion of humility in these verses by pointing the finger at two attitudes guaranteed to kill a relationship: "Do nothing out of selfish ambition or vain

Principle #5: The Greatest Are the Servants

conceit ..." (Philippians 2:3a). Selfish ambition—What will I *get*? Vain conceit—How will I *look*? It's obvious that these attitudes are deadly, but God in his kindness often reminds us of the obvious. He knows that just because we know something doesn't mean we do it. At their core, relationships are about giving, not getting—and that's why selfish ambition is so destructive to relationships. I've known couples who decided to have a child in the hope that they would get their emotional needs met. Train wreck ahead! Remember this too: self-focused

Humility is being honest about who you are and about who God is— about his strength, his goodness, and what he can do in your life.

conceit is equally destructive to relationships. Some people wear their relationships like a flashy gold bracelet. "Look who I'm with!" You can be sure relationships bathed in conceit will not grow.

Humility Is the Daily Decision to Humble Yourself under God's Mighty Hand

Peter declares, "God opposes the proud but gives grace to the humble. Humble yourselves, therefore, under God's mighty hand, that he may lift you up in due time" (1 Peter 5:5–6). Humility is not putting yourself down; it's lifting God up. Humility is being honest about who you are—about your strengths and weaknesses, and it is being honest about who God is—about his strength, his goodness, and what he can do in your life.

To encourage you in the daily struggle to display genuine

humility in your life, I invite you to write the following words on a card and put it where you can read it several times a day:

> *Humility is not thinking less of myself;*
>   *it is thinking more of others.*
> *Humility is not putting myself down;*
>   *it is lifting God up.*
> *Humility is not denying my strengths;*
>   *it is being openly honest about my weaknesses.*
> *Humility is seeing that without Christ I can do nothing,*
>   *but in Christ I can do all things!*

With these truths in mind, do two simple things. As you go through your day, admit you are proud, and act humble. Who doesn't struggle with pride? I certainly do. *So just admit it.* Pride constantly invades our thoughts and too often guides our words and reactions. And then *act humble.* Don't wait until you feel humble; just choose to act humble. Isn't that being hypocritical? No, it's being obedient. God commands you to act with humility, so it's the right decision, no matter what you may be feeling. In fact, don't even try to *feel* humble. Humility is not aware of itself, and if you are trying to feel humble, you're going to become so aware of yourself that you are not humble anymore. Here's the trap you can fall into: you try to feel humble and may even start to feel a little humble — and then you get proud of the fact that you feel a little humble, and you're not humble anymore. Don't try to feel humble — it's spiritual quicksand; just act humble. Humility is throwing your selfishness away in complete concern for someone else. Act humble.

Pride is ugly. It would be simple to allow yourself to

wallow in discouragement over what you have suffered because of your pride. Don't do it! If you do, your pride is still the focus — even if it's a negative focus. Your pride will still be in control. If you want to be great, decide to act humble and trust that God wants to do something in your life only he can do.

The Daily Greatness Quiz

Look back at the four parts of the daily greatness quiz we've learned about over the past six days — how humility handles our ambition, our need to be noticed, our tendency to compare, and our relationship with God — and ask these questions:

> What ambition can I give to God this week?
>
> Whose need must I begin to notice this week?
>
> Where do I need to honor God, even if I am in the lowest seat? Or trust him, even if I am in the highest seat?
>
> Have I started to make faith a do-it-yourself burden? How can I choose to express fresh trust in God?

Imagine for just a moment the incredible freedom of humility — being set free from the need to be noticed, from worrying about which seat you are sitting in or not sitting in. Being set free to trust God and to live out his ambition for your life. Real freedom!

As we conclude this week's look at the principle "The greatest are the servants," I invite you to join me in this prayer:

Lord, it's hard for me to care about others. It's a lot easier to care about myself. It's just easier to care about what I can accomplish and how I am being recognized and how I compare. But you've shown the way. If I exalt myself, I miss out on your best. When I humble myself, Lord, I discover that you're able to give a strength and a power through depending on you that I do not and cannot have on my own. Apart from Christ I can do nothing, but in Christ I can do all things! In Jesus' name I pray. Amen.

DAY THIRTY-FIVE
Thinking about My Relationships

Point to Ponder: Don't try to feel humble; act humble.

Verse to Remember: *I can do all things through Christ who strengthens me* (Philippians 4:13 NKJV).

Question to Consider: Is there an ugly point of pride that I have been ignoring in my life?

Tomorrow: The big question

Treat Others as You Want Them to Treat You

Do to others as you would have them do to you.

Luke 6:31

The Big Question

In all we've heard from Jesus about relationships, we've often come back to one place in his ministry — a hillside beside the Sea of Galilee. Jesus sat on the green hills gently sloping up from the blue waters of Galilee and delivered the most famous sermon ever spoken — the Sermon on the Mount. It is a sermon filled with truth about healthy relationships with God and with each other.

We turn again to these words of Jesus as we begin our look at the final relationship principle. It is a familiar principle, one many of us learned as children, but in that familiarity we can easily miss its power and impact.

Jesus said, "Do for others what you would like them to do for you" (Matthew 7:12 NLT). We call this the "Golden Rule." Think of the powerful potential for change in this one rule! If we could begin to think and act in sync with this one rule in our relationships, the difference would be radical.

Yet lurking off to the side of this life-changing principle is a big question. Whether we like it or not, this question makes its way into each of our relationships. We can try to push it out of our mind, thinking it's too selfish a question — but it's still there. The only way to really deal with this question is not to ignore it but to face it and answer it.

The question is this: "How do I get *my* needs met in this relationship?"

As unselfish as we may become, we still have needs — and we wonder how these needs will get met.

Here is a big answer to this big question: "I must give myself to meeting others' needs if I'm to get my needs met!" The only way to get my selfish needs met is to be unselfish. Without exception clauses or limiting statements, Jesus says, "Do for others what you would like them to do for you." This is the rule that will fuel any relationship. It is the rule that will meet the needs of both you and others in your relationships.

> The only way to get your selfish needs met is to be unselfish.

For such a simple statement, the Golden Rule has gathered an amazingly varied attention over the years. In the sphere of government, the Roman emperor Alexander Severus, who ruled from AD 222 to 235, adopted the Golden Rule as his motto and had it inscribed in gold on the walls of his palace. It has since been placed on countless buildings of legislature and law. In the sphere of religion, some form of the Golden Rule appears in most of the world's religions. In philosophy, apologist G. K. Chesterton and his anti-Christian friend George Bernard Shaw engaged in a famous debate over the meaning of the Golden Rule, with Shaw concluding, "The Golden Rule is that there is no Golden Rule," and Chesterton replying, "That there is no Golden Rule [would itself be] a

Golden Rule."* In the business world, J. C. Penney expressed his commitment to the Golden Rule by naming his first department store in 1902 the "Golden Rule Store"—a name adopted by all his stores until 1913 when the chain became known as "J. C. Penney."

As interesting as this attention may be, the true meaning of the Golden Rule isn't seen in an inscription on a building or in a philosophical discussion; its true meaning is expressed when a husband sees himself through his wife's eyes and says, "Please forgive me for my selfishness and insensitivity," or when a friend meets a need no one else has even noticed. Its meaning is seen best in the way we choose to relate to one another.

When it comes to this issue of getting our needs met in a relationship, we often play by rules different from the Golden Rule—rules we may have learned while growing up or developed out of our own life experiences. Whatever the source, these man-made rules sometimes seem to work well at the beginning but spoil the relationship in the end.

One of our relational rules is the *Reciprocal Rule*: "Whatever you do for me, that's what I'll do for you; you scratch my back, and I'll scratch yours." Many play by this rule. It may well be our most popular rule as we work to make our relationships successful. There is certainly nothing wrong with returning a kindness that has been done to you—but this rule is really about our assumption that we've *earned* a kindness because we've been kind to someone else. In the end it is a rule based on selfishness, not service. If this rule is all we have, relationships can easily degenerate into waiting for

---

*Quoted in G. K. Chesterton, *The Collected Works of G. K. Chesterton*, vol. 1 (Fort Collins, Colo.: Ignatius, 1986), 67.

the other person to make the first move before we reciprocate. This kind of rule isn't powerful enough to give us the relationships that God created us to enjoy.

We also have the *Ricochet Rule*: "Do to someone based on what some other person has done to you. The way I've been treated in other relationships controls the way I treat you in our relationship." This rule frequently invades a marriage. The way your parents treated you is determining the way you're treating your spouse. The way a former spouse treated you or even the way your kids treated you strongly influences the way you're treating your spouse. You've had a rough day at work, and you take it out on your family. This rule underlies the old story about the man who comes home after a lousy day at work and takes it out on his wife by firing angry words at her. His wife then speaks harshly to one of the children, the child walks away and kicks the dog, and the dog bites the head off of a Barbie doll lying on the floor. It would have saved them all a lot of pain if the man had just come home and bitten the head off the Barbie doll!

Then we have the *Hidden Motive Rule*: "I act like I'm doing it for you, but it's really to get what I want." Most of us see through this one quite easily. This rule is at work in the husband who lovingly gives his wife a new necklace right before he tells her about the new fishing boat he just purchased without her knowledge.

All of our games and rules pale alongside the simple words of Jesus. *The Message* paraphrase of the Bible states it, "Here is a simple, rule-of-thumb guide for behavior: Ask yourself what you want people to do for you, then grab the initiative and do it for *them*" (Matthew 7:12). Want to transform your relationships? That's the simple rule.

The Golden Rule is easy to say and to understand; it lends itself well to memorization. But how do we go beyond these just being good words? How do you begin to actually *live* this rule in your relationships? If you're ever going to get there, you must deal with what you do when you sense that your needs are not being met in a relationship.

We've all been there. Instead of applying the Golden Rule, we get into a standoff: "You didn't meet my needs, so I'm not meeting your needs." We get into a downward spiral — with a spouse, a child, a parent, a friend. Maybe you would balk at the word *stubborn*, but if you look deep into your heart, there's stubbornness at work — probably in both of you — that says, "I'm not going to be the first one to give in! I'm going to make sure you go first. It's your turn. I went first the last five times." Consider this question: "Do you see anything about 'turns' in the Golden Rule?" Well, come to think about it, there is something about whose turn it is to meet another's need — it's always *my* turn. "Ask yourself what you want people to do for you, then grab the initiative and do it for *them*."

When you find yourself stuck in one of those places where neither person in the relationship wants to meet the other's need, what can you do? How can you turn your heart around so that your relationship can grow?

Thankfully, there is a way to break the logjam. You can begin by thanking God for the other person. Find something — even a small thing — about them for which you can be thankful. I've found that I cannot act unselfishly toward someone unless I am thankful for them. It just doesn't work. Your heart is opened to meet others' needs when you are thankful for them.

Thinking about My Relationships

Point to Ponder: I must give myself to meeting others' needs if I'm going to get my own needs met.

Verse to Remember: *"Do for others what you would like them to do for you"* (Matthew 7:12 NLT).

Question to Consider: Who can I thank God for so that I can grab the initiative in meeting his or her needs?

Tomorrow: Love is sacrificial

37

Love Is Sacrificial

EXPERIENCE THE TRUTH

Jesus hangs in tortured pain on the cross. His back, whipped and scourged, presses against the rough wood. His hands and feet throb with the pain of the piercing nails. His eyes sting and blur from blood that runs from a head pierced with a crown of thorns. His chest aches as he gasps for air.

Below him stand the leaders who have just made the political deal that condemns him to this torture. They are laughing. They gloat as they gaze at their trophy—the Son of God on the cross. They mock Jesus in his pain, challenging him to come down from the cross. Jesus knew the reason they had campaigned for his crucifixion. Their actions did not spring from confusion or misunderstanding. They were jealous of the attention being given to Jesus—jealousy that had grown into a

fear of losing their position. These leaders were Jesus'
enemies. And these enemies had condemned him to
death.

Jesus hears their ridicule through his pain and
chooses to pray a simple prayer: "Father, forgive them."
Jesus did not just talk about love for enemies; he chose
to love his enemies even as they wounded him.

Based on Luke 23:26-43

The Golden Rule is a picture of the true nature of love.
Love is not reciprocal; love is sacrificial. Love gives itself
without waiting for others to give.

I have to admit that I don't have the power to love like this.
I don't have it in me to love my enemies—I have a hard enough
time loving my friends! If you join me in this admission, don't
despair. In the very moment you think something is impossible,
you may find the opportunity of a lifetime. Jesus gives you
truth to empower you: what is humanly impossible is possible
with God (Luke 18:27). What you cannot do in your strength
you can do through the strength that God alone can give.
Jesus gave you these commands not to discourage you but to
invite you to trust in him for a kind of love you could never
manufacture on your own.

Jesus encourages us by pointing to two amazing benefits
to living out his Golden Rule: "Your reward from heaven will
be very great, and you will truly be acting as children of the
Most High" (Luke 6:35 NLT). There's great reward in living
the way God wants you to live—and some of this reward is
enjoyed in this world, while the vast majority awaits you in

heaven. And by living life God's way, your relationship with God as his child will be obvious to those who watch you. The world needs to see sacrificial love. The world needs to see us as followers of Jesus who act in sacrificial love for each another, the world around us, and even our enemies.

My friends in Rwanda encourage me to express sacrificial love. In training pastors and working with churches there, I've met many who've had all or most of their family killed in the genocide that devastated that country in 1994. The stories don't come out quickly, and they are always painful to tell and to hear. Yet they almost always end with forgiveness—a son choosing to forgive the neighbors who killed his family, a father choosing to forgive the ones who brought about the deaths of his wife and children. Nothing anyone could do could provide restitution for their grief and loss, yet they are choosing to love sacrificially.

The need to receive God's power to live the Golden Rule is clearly seen as Jesus continued his sermon that day. After talking to the crowd about the challenge of loving their enemies, he told them: "Try to show as much compassion as your Father does" (Luke 6:36 LB).

The world needs to see sacrificial love.

This takes our responsibility to a whole new level. My relationship with others is molded not merely by what I want but by the example God provides. I'm not only to think about how I want to be treated; I'm to look at *how God treats people.* If I'm going to live out this action of sacrificial love, it's not going to happen accidentally. It's going to take a step—a conscious decision to act toward others the way God acts toward me.

As I write these words, I have some feelings you may relate

to. I see a lot of reasons why the principles taught by Jesus shouldn't work in the real world—the unlovable people we sometimes encounter, the times this kind of sacrificial love has been misunderstood, the intense emotions in ourselves that we stumble over, our own lack of willpower, and the inadequacy of our inner resources. There are a hundred reasons why this kind of love just will not work.

And there is one reason why it will: *Jesus*. The life Jesus lived tells us that this is the kind of love that will change the world. Jesus is willing to give us the power to love the way he loved.

How can you take the Golden Rule from platitude to attitude? Two things have to happen. First of all, *someone has to make a way for you; someone has to give you the power.* Jesus has already taken care of that. He came to this earth and taught us to love in a new way. He wouldn't have taught it if he wasn't willing to give us the power to live it. Don't let your imperfections keep you from starting on this path; don't let the fact that you'll never get it perfectly while on this earth keep you from staying on this path to the end of your life. Jesus provides the open door to get started—and he will provide the power to keep you going your whole journey through.

The Golden Rule finds an echo in the writings of many world religions, philosophers, and poets. "What is so different, so powerful, about these words of Jesus?" you may ask. Here it is in a nutshell: *only Jesus can give the power* to do what he taught us to do. When he commands us, "Do for others what you would like them to do for you," there is an implied promise that he will give you the power to do just that.

The second thing that has to happen is this: we've got to

make a decision to *take the first step* on that path. You can be standing in front of a plane bound for Africa with the ticket in your hands, but until you step on that plane, you're not going anywhere. You can be standing in front of Jesus and hear him say, "Here's how I want you to live. Here's what I want to give you the power to do. Take the first step. Watch what I can do in your life"—but until you trust him with your fears, you're not going anywhere. We all have fears—no question about it. Who isn't afraid to love like this? Who isn't afraid to stumble? God's love is greater—so much greater—than all your fears. If you never take the first step, you'll never experience how much greater his love truly is.

DAY THIRTY-SEVEN
Thinking about My Relationships

Point to Ponder: Love is not reciprocal; love is sacrificial.

Verse to Remember: *"Try to show as much compassion as your Father does"* (Luke 6:36 LB).

Question to Consider: What have I found that helps me get my eyes off the reasons sacrificial love won't work and on the only one who can motivate a new kind of love in me?

Tomorrow: Love your enemies

33

Love Your Enemies

If you're anything like me, the words of Jesus we'll reflect on today will challenge you to your core—maybe even to the point that you'll want to set them aside and settle for a lesser kind of love, a love that is comforting but not life changing. Yet something in us just cannot settle for what we know to be less—not when we know that Jesus offers something more. I encourage you to remember what we looked at yesterday: sacrificial love can only be empowered by Jesus.

Jesus taught this about love:

> "If you love those who love you, what credit is that to you? Even 'sinners' love those who love them. And if you do good to those who are good to you, what credit is that to you? Even 'sinners' do that. And if you lend to those from whom you expect repayment, what credit is that to you? Even 'sinners' lend to 'sinners,' expecting to be repaid in full. But love your enemies, do good to them."
>
> Luke 6:32-35

If you act in love toward only those who do the same for you, you really aren't doing anything extraordinary. Jesus taught that the Golden Rule is not golden unless it applies to *everyone*—which, of course, includes your enemies.

The first and greatest commandment is to love God. The second commandment is to love your neighbor. The new commandment is to love one another. And the Golden Rule means you love even your enemies. God, neighbor, one another, enemies—this covers everyone!

To love your enemies really widens the circle of your love. Jesus doesn't say you have to *like* everything your enemies do. There may be actions your enemies take that you abhor. Love doesn't mean "like." You don't have to put your arm around an enemy and say, "You're my buddy." Love means you practice the Golden Rule toward that person; you treat him as you would want to be treated.

"OK, love an enemy. Tough to do, but I'll work on it," we say to ourselves. But then Jesus gets specific. He gives us pictures of what he means. Earlier in the Sermon on the Mount, Jesus zeroed in on how we typically treat our personal enemies:

> "You have heard that the law of Moses says, 'If an eye is injured, injure the eye of the person who did it. If a tooth gets knocked out, knock out the tooth of the person who did it.' But I say, don't resist an evil person! If you are slapped on the right cheek, turn the other, too. If you are ordered to court and your shirt is taken from you, give your coat, too. If a soldier demands that you carry his gear for a mile, carry it two miles. Give to those who ask, and don't turn away from those who want to borrow."
>
> Matthew 5:38-42 NLT

"An eye for an eye, and a tooth for a tooth," or "Treat others as you would have them treat you" — two very different ways of life.

The words of Jesus in these verses are so challenging that it's difficult to get our minds around them. The immediate temptation is to change the subject and get the attention off us! Some focus on Jesus' words as referring more to nations as enemies than to personal enemies — which, of course, misses the point. These verses are all about things that are very personal — a slap on the cheek, a shirt that is taken, a pack carried on your back. A discussion about what the Bible has to say about war is a valuable thing, yet I fear that in our attempt to take these verses in that direction, we lose the personal and relational meaning Jesus obviously intended. These verses deal not with broad and complex geopolitical issues but with straightforward and hurtful personal issues.

Relationships often do not go the way we want them to go. Jesus' way of righting a wrong is not to act in revenge but to follow the Golden Rule. Instead of counseling resistance or rejection or reprisal, Jesus challenges us to treat other people as we would want to be treated. Jesus taught that the Golden Rule must be applied not only when relationships are going right but also when they are going wrong.

Jesus pictures in these verses what it means to love an enemy. For most people, these words of Jesus initially raise some questions — questions that can lead us toward a new level of love. Jesus talks about an insulting slap on the cheek. When Jesus says, "Turn the other, too," we scratch our heads in wonder. "Does this mean I have to let someone injure me?" "Does this mean a child cannot defend himself at school?" "Does this mean Christians are OK with being seen as spineless cowards?" Look at the example of Jesus, who overturned tables and drove out those who were taking financial advantage of others at the temple (John 2:14–16)—not exactly in sync with any "just take whatever anyone wants to do to you" version of Matthew 5:38–42.

Whenever I have problems understanding a difficult biblical passage, the vast majority of the time it is due to my own presuppositions and cultural baggage. Jesus points to situations where you are insulted—where you are slapped on one cheek—not to situations where you're threatened by the actions of a bully on the playground or a thief breaking into your house or a violent, abusive spouse. In Jesus' culture, a slap to the right cheek was clearly understood to mean a slap with the back of the hand—twice as insulting as a slap with an open palm. When Jesus tells us to turn the other cheek, the meaning is abundantly clear: instead of choosing revenge, we must choose love. Revenge slaps the other person back; love turns the other cheek, with the hope that it will wake him up and cause him to change. But even if he doesn't change, you have decided not to allow his insult to turn you into an insulting person. You have chosen to love. Jesus is encouraging an act of courage, not cowardice. The Golden Rule is a decision for *vulnerable love.*

Jesus challenges us to treat other people as we would want to be treated.

Jesus also talks about someone who wants to sue you and take your shirt. When Jesus says, "Give your coat, too," he shows how much he values relationships over possessions. He is not talking about legal cases between businesses; he is talking about relationships. We miss the power and the personal impact of Jesus' teaching when we get into philosophical debates beyond the bounds of what he is discussing. He is talking about relationships and telling us that a spirit of vengeance or bitterness is much too high a price to pay for the loss of a shirt. And that the gift of a coat is not too great a price to pay for even the possibility of a restored relationship. The Golden Rule is a decision for *generous love*.

Jesus next talks about a soldier of an occupying army demanding that you, a civilian, carry his gear for a mile. When Jesus says, "Carry it two miles," he is encouraging us to personalize the demand with the surprising response of sacrifice. When an opponent tries to take from you, decide to give to them. The Golden Rule is a decision for *sacrificial love*.

Jesus then talks about giving to someone who wants to borrow from you. That's much too simple, much too clear, much too convicting! The Golden Rule is a decision for *practical love*.

Jesus piles example on example because he knew we'd have a tough time getting this concept. We like to believe we can take some measure of revenge against a person who has hurt us without it affecting our soul or refuse to help someone who asks with no impact on our hearts. Jesus, who knows us better than we know ourselves, tells us it isn't so.

In all of these examples, Jesus teaches the same thing: When someone is trying to take from you, surprise them and decide to give to them. Instead of becoming protective or vindictive, decide to love. "But isn't that being a codependent enabler?" you may ask. "Should I let people walk all over me?" Of course not. Jesus isn't talking about allowing someone to control you. Quite the opposite. He is encouraging you to stay in control of the situation by choosing to act in radical love toward someone, even if they treat you as an enemy. God did not create you to be codependent or to be independent; he created you to be dependent on him.

Jesus is showing us that we have a relationship even with an enemy. He teaches us that the only way to win over our enemy is by doing good—and it's the only way to keep our spiritual dignity in a difficult situation as well. Instead of allowing our enemy to take our rights away, we choose to give to them.

Begin with one relationship and one decision today.

Instead of trying to apply the Golden Rule to every relationship in your life for the rest of your life all at once, begin with one relationship and one decision today. Know this: when you make the slightest choice to love in this way, it is a choice to *be like God*: "Love your enemies and pray for those who persecute you, that you may be sons of your Father in heaven. He causes his sun to rise on the evil and the good, and sends rain on the righteous and the unrighteous" (Matthew 5:44–45).

Let this truth encourage you as you apply the Golden Rule, one small step at a time: God has carried out the Golden Rule like no other, and he graciously shows us how it is done. He loved us when we were still his enemies. Paul tells us, "God demonstrates his own love for us in this: While we were still sinners, Christ died for us" (Romans 5:8). Jesus came to earth and did for us what we couldn't do for ourselves. He did it "while we were still sinners"—while we were still rejecting God's plan and living our own selfish lives. There is no better example of loving your enemies than God's love for you.

Jesus can teach this because Jesus lived it:

- He took more than a slap to the face; he took the insults hurled at him on the cross.
- No one sued for his shirt; it was stripped from his back, and soldiers gambled for the right to take it home.
- He was not compelled to carry a soldier's gear a mile down a country road; he was forced to bear through the streets of Jerusalem the cross on which he would die.

Jesus possessed all the rights of God in human flesh, but he did not demand those rights. Those who opposed him did not take his rights from him; he gave himself willingly. He loved us when we were his enemies.

DAY THIRTY-EIGHT
Thinking about My Relationships

Point to Ponder: When someone is trying to take from you, surprise them and decide to give to them.

Verse to Remember: *God demonstrates his own love for us in this: While we were still sinners, Christ died for us* (Romans 5:8).

Question to Consider: Have I asked God for the strength to act with love toward someone who is treating me as an enemy?

Tomorrow: Forget the ideal, go for the real

39

Forget the Ideal,
Go for the Real

Our temptation to hang on to an idealized picture of relationships can easily keep us from genuine joy in a relationship. An
idealized family evening would look something like this:

You get home from work at exactly 5:15 — because the
freeways once again parted like the Red Sea for you on your
drive home. Everyone rushes to meet you at the door — even
your golden retriever.

The whole family pitches in to make dinner. It's pasta night
at your house, so one of the kids gets out the pasta maker to
make fresh pasta, another puts the homemade bread in the
oven, and you go out to the garden to pick the tomatoes and
spices for the sauce.

During the meal you have a scintillating conversation in
which everyone shares the experiences of the day — and their
deepest feelings about every one of those experiences. Then
you clean up together — it takes all of about two and a half
minutes. While the kids finish their homework (with *no* help
from you required!), you go to the woodshop to work on the

handcrafted dining table and chairs you're building. You are carving scenes from the life of Jesus onto the back of each chair. (The detailed faces of each person in the feeding of the five thousand are taking you a while.)

After everyone has finished their homework, you gather for family entertainment. Instead of playing board games or gardening together as usual, tonight you're making a movie for the local PBS station on the wonder of family life. You laugh, you cry, you hug—it's sure to win an Emmy. The kids then all go to bed, and you bring out the candles for a wonderful romantic evening. You and your wife make romantic, passionate love for the tenth night in a row—then read a Bible passage together and fall asleep in each other's arms.

> *Take the only life you've got—your ordinary, real life—and give it to God.*

Ha! Here's the more likely reality: You get home at 7:30 after fighting two hours of traffic, eat a cold piece of pizza, try to help one of your kids with algebra—a subject you last understood in 1983—then grab the remote control and channel surf your way to sleep. Your romantic evening is your spouse punching you in the arm and saying, "Hey, you fell asleep in the chair again. Stop snoring."

The goal of love is not some false ideal we've conjured up in our minds; the goal of love is *seeing God at work* in our real lives. Why is it so important that we get rid of these visions of the ideal life? Because our idealized images actually keep us from experiencing the great things God wants to do in our relationships. We always have less than the ideal—so we're never satisfied; we know we can't reach the ideal—so we just give up. The false image we've built up in our minds keeps us from the real thing.

Back in the Old Testament, we read a lot about people worshiping idols. People trusted these false gods made out of wood or stone to give them a better life, better health, a better family. We don't have little wooden gods anymore. But we still have idols.

We make an idol out of the ideal. We set up in our minds a perfect image of how things should be—and end up focusing on that. It keeps us from the real thing. This idol keeps us from making the little changes that can make a huge difference.

Paul tells us where the real thing starts: "So here's what I want you to do, God helping you: Take your everyday, ordinary life—your sleeping, eating, going-to-work, and walking-around life—and place it before God as an offering. Embracing what God does for you is the best thing you can do for him" (Romans 12:1 MSG).

Take the only life you've got—your ordinary, real life—and give it to God. Ask God to help you to love in a new kind of way. Stop waiting for some ideal vision to come true in your life, and just begin to love. Love now!

Here are some examples of love in the real world:

- Neil and Robin (we talked about them on Day 1 of this forty-day journey) did this. In spite of Robin's lifelong struggles caused by an aneurysm, they both decided to love now. Life is not ideal, yet their love is real.
- Paul and Teri did this. Faced with huge personal and business debt after an economic downturn, they decided to work their way out together instead of blaming each other. Life is not ideal, yet their love is real.

- John and Cheryl did this. After years of watching John's alcoholism destroy him even as he succeeded professionally, Cheryl confronted John with his need to change. Recovery wasn't easy and didn't come in an instant, but John began to work through the steps to healing. He now leads others toward change through Celebrate Recovery—a Christ-centered recovery program. Life is not ideal, yet their love is real.
- Erik did this in his relationship with his dad. Growing up under constant ridicule and physical threat from his father, Erik could have bitterly rejected him in return. Instead, he chose to forgive and to be at peace in the relationship. Life is not perfect, yet his love is real.
- Paul and Janine did this. Their daughter died at birth, and they were told they couldn't have another child. They could have chosen a path of quiet depression, but instead they decided to pour out their love by adopting. Life is not perfect, yet their love is real.
- Dee did this. Left with five children to love and raise after her husband died in an accident, she wondered where to turn. God's people served her, God's presence surrounded her like a warm blanket, and God's plan and promise gave her a hope for the future. Life is far from ideal; God's love is awesomely real.

The circumstances of your life are not perfect. You are not perfect. The people you love are not perfect. But God *is* perfect. So instead of trying to perfect the imperfectable, choose to focus on praising the one who is perfect. And then, bolstered by that praise, choose real love.

Thinking about My Relationships

Point to Ponder: We make an idol out of the ideal.

Verse to Remember: *So here's what I want you to do, God helping you: Take your everyday, ordinary life—your sleeping, eating, going-to-work, and walking-around life—and place it before God as an offering. Embracing what God does for you is the best thing you can do for him* (Romans 12:1 MSG).

Question to Consider: Has some idealized image been keeping me from the great things God wants to do in my life and relationships?

Tomorrow: The relationship principles of Jesus

40

The Relationship Principles of Jesus

Any time you can walk alongside an expert, you have an opportunity to learn and change. For the past forty days, we've walked alongside Jesus, focusing on what we can learn from him about relationships.

We've seen the priority that Jesus puts on relationships. In response to the question, "Of all of the commandments, which is the most important?" Jesus replied, "The most important commandment is this: ... 'you must love the Lord your God with all your heart, all your soul, all your mind, and all your strength.' The second is equally important: 'Love your neighbor as yourself.' No other commandment is greater than these" (Mark 12:29–31 NLT).

We've seen Jesus in the upper room with his disciples. He knew he was going to die the next day, and so he chose his last words in those last moments to communicate something he wanted them to never forget: "A new command I give you: Love one another. As I have loved you, so you must love one another" (John 13:34).

We've seen Jesus traveling the dusty roads, talking with honesty and love to both his greatest enemies and his closest friends. Pharisees and disciples alike—Jesus communicated clearly from the heart to all he encountered. He exemplified the truth he taught: "Out of the overflow of the heart the mouth speaks" (Matthew 12:34).

We've heard Jesus talking about planks and specks in the eye as he taught us, "Do not judge, or you too will be judged" (Matthew 7:1). He showed us that hypocrisy can be replaced by integrity and mercy.

We've heard Jesus continually reminding his status-conscious disciples that the path to genuine greatness is humble service: "The greatest among you will be your servant. For whoever exalts himself will be humbled, and whoever humbles himself will be exalted" (Matthew 23:11–12). He challenged us with the truth that God's plan begins with simple dependence: "Whoever humbles himself like this child is the greatest in the kingdom of heaven" (Matthew 18:4).

What would life look like if you began to live out in all your relationships this kind of love Jesus taught?

We've seen Jesus calling us to follow the rule that will strengthen any relationship—the Golden Rule: "Do to others what you would have them do to you" (Luke 6:31). Jesus himself modeled the true nature of sacrificial love—loving his enemies and giving himself for us on the cross.

You may have tried to love like this, only to find yourself coming up short. Don't let the fact that you stumbled in the first leg keep you from finishing the race. You have to stumble before you walk and walk before you run. And even once you get your pace, you'll still find yourself stumbling at times.

I invite you to set aside all those thoughts crowding your mind with reasons why you can't apply these relationship principles of Jesus. For just a moment, open your mind to faith, and dream with me. What would life look like if you began to live out in all your relationships this kind of love Jesus taught?

Place the highest value on relationships. Imagine someone saying to you, "Without a friend like you, I wouldn't have made it through." Imagine your grown kids looking you in the eye and saying, "No matter how busy you were when we were growing up, I always knew I was more important than any project or job."

Love as Jesus loves you. Imagine a new power to love in a new way. Imagine relationships with other followers of Jesus that give a glimpse of the awesome love of Jesus.

Communicate from the heart. Imagine yourself saying the kind of words that drop like pebbles in a lake and ripple out to change for the better the whole atmosphere of your home or office. Imagine your husband or wife whispering the words, "Thank you for being honest about how you felt. Our marriage would never be this great if you hadn't shared with me the feelings you were struggling with during that time years ago."

As you judge, you will be judged. Imagine a coworker saying, "When everyone else was laughing at me behind my back, you offered real compassion and understanding. I don't know much yet about this Jesus you follow and try to imitate, but I do know I want what you have."

The greatest are the servants. Imagine yourself standing

in the presence of Jesus and hearing the words, "Well done, good and faithful servant."

Treat others as you want them to treat you. Imagine a friend coming to you and saying, "When you gave me that hug or brought me that meal or sent me that note last year or …, you'll never know how that one act of kindness changed my life. Things have never been the same since that moment."

As we end this journey together, I invite you to pray this prayer with me:

Jesus, in my own power I can't love this way! Show me how—and then give me the strength. I need more than your example; I need your power. I humbly ask for your power. Lord, I want to love the way you loved. As crazy a dream as that is, as high a goal as that sets, I commit myself to spend the rest of my life pursuing it. I want to be like you, Jesus. I want to love like you, Jesus. Thank you from the depths of my soul for loving me. In your name. Amen.

Questions for Friends, Couples, and Small Groups

Place the Highest Value on Relationships

1. What do some of the popular songs about love say about our common beliefs about love?

2. Does it bother you when you see the potential of your relationships and you're nowhere near meeting it? What do you do with this feeling?

3. In Jesus' story of the Good Samaritan, which seems the greater risk to you: helping in the immediate crisis, or coming back to follow up? Why?

4. How do you make love the highest priority when there is so much to do in your life?

5. Who is the most loving person you have ever known? How did they show love to others?

6. In what relationship(s) do you need to show more of God's love? What would be a practical first step?

Love as Jesus Loves You

1. What needs to change in your life in order to create margin and give you time to love as Jesus loved?

2. Can you remember times when you acted in love, even though you didn't feel loving at the time? What helped you to follow through on the desire to act in love?

3. How could your discussion group encourage you as you seek to allow God to take a love that is old and make it new?

4. What does it look like for you to shift from trying to make things happen in your own power to trusting in God's power for your relationships?

5. What project(s) could your discussion group do together to show practical love?

Communicate from the Heart

1. When it comes to conflict, are you a skunk or a turtle? (A turtle hides his or her head at the sign of trouble, while a skunk lets everyone know how he or she feels.)

2. Describe a time when you were helped by someone who was honest and loving enough to tell you what you *needed* to hear rather than just what you *wanted* to hear. Or was there a time in your life when you wished somebody would have done that?

3. Is there someone in your life you need to confront? Someone you need to encourage?

4. How could you be better at building trust with your words?

5. Did the way Jesus pictured the truth with Nicodemus and the woman at the well give you any ideas for using pictures to get the point across in your conversations?

WEEK 4
As You Judge, You Will Be Judged

1. When have you been offered forgiveness, and what did it mean to you?

2. What are some misconceptions about forgiveness?

3. How does God's forgiveness for you strengthen you in your daily life?

4. Is there someone you need to forgive or someone you need to ask for forgiveness?

5. How willing are you to forgive? Why is it hard to forgive?

6. How can the group pray for you in the areas of hypocrisy, integrity, and mercy?

The Greatest Are the Servants

1. How have your relationships been affected by these last four weeks of looking at Jesus' love?

2. Give an example of when someone did something unselfish for you.

3. How is selfishness the enemy of strong relationships? How does service strengthen relationships?

4. As you think about Jesus' story of those seeking the highest seats at the banquet table, have you ever been willing to take the lowest place? Tell the group what happened when you did.

5. Have you had an opportunity to serve someone together as a group? What did God do for your heart as you served?

WEEK 6

Treat Others as You Want Them to Treat You

1. Is there something practical you can do to develop a habit of treating others as you would want them to treat you?

2. How can you begin to "forget the ideal and go for the real" in a relationship?

3. What does Jesus' Golden Rule say to you about what you could do for someone in a relationship this week?

4. What is the greatest lesson you have learned in the last six weeks that is helping you to depend on Christ's strength to love others? Who else in your circle of relationships could you pass these new insights on to?

Bible Versions

Putting It Together Again When It's All Fallen Apart

7 Principles for Rebuilding Your Life

Tom Holladay

Life crises can throw you into a tail-spin—a lost job, a failed relationship, a struggling business, a financial mess. Where do you start? How do you pull it together? How do you begin again?

Tom Holladay experienced a catastrophe first-hand when a sudden flood in California destroyed his home, his church, and the homes of many church members. Tom and his congregation had to rebuild, and they used the principles in the book of Nehemiah to get back on their feet.

Now a teaching pastor at Saddleback Church, Tom will help you discover seven principles for putting it together again that will give you the direction you need to get rolling on that fresh start. Holladay will walk you through seeing every problem as an opportunity, facing the obstacles head on and taking your first step, knowing how to expect and reject opposition, build on your success, and dedicating yourself to the One who rebuilds our souls.

The task of starting again can seem impossible. And sometimes you just need to rebuild your confidence and regain a sense of purpose. If you're trying to find the emotional energy, but you just don't have it in you, let Holladay encourage you. He understands how difficult and rewarding the business of rebuilding is. This book is your encouraging how-to guide to starting again and stepping into a better future.

Available wherever books are sold!